THE NATURE NOVEL FROM HARDY TO LAWRENCE

THE NATURE NOVEL
FROM HARDY TO
LAWRENCE

JOHN ALCORN
Professor of English Literature
San Francisco State University

First edition 1977
Reprinted 1978, 1980

Published by
THE MACMILLAN PRESS LTD
London and Basingstoke
Associated companies in Delhi Dublin Hong Kong
Johannesburg Lagos Melbourne New York
Singapore Tokyo

ISBN 0 333 21195 2

Printed in Hong Kong

Contents

Naturam expellas furca, tamen usque recurret
You may drive out nature with a fork, but she will
always return.

Horace, *Epistles*, I. x. 24

Preface

The aim of this study is to demonstrate that between Thomas Hardy and D. H. Lawrence there arose in English literature a new story-telling convention, a convention which involved new themes, descriptive techniques, plot devices, methods of characterization, and new ways of relating character to landscape; and that these changes, far from being gratuitous or accidental, reflect a single basic insight about human experience, an insight which continues to make its force felt in English and American fiction in our own time.

The scope of this subject is necessarily broad, covering some dozen writers and reaching across several decades. But the formal aim is specific and confined: to trace a continuity of theme and technique in a group of English novels during the first two decades of the twentieth century. It is not my aim to provide a rounded or total picture of the novel during this period, but rather to center upon a single literary impulse which co-existed with several others. Thus if I seem to neglect such major novelists as Conrad, James, or Joyce, it is because they relate only occasionally to my subject. Even in respect to the literature which lies within the bounds of my subject, I have had to be highly selective, since the body of that literature is very large. Much more might have been said, for example, about such writers as Wilfrid Scawen Blunt or R. B. Cunninghame Graham; instead I have treated analogous material in the works of W. H. Hudson and H. M. Tomlinson. My method has been to select writers and books which seemed most effectively to represent a huge library of material, much of it now unread and forgotten. The importance of this body of literature is in large measure a cumulative one: taken together, these works provide a new perspective for twentieth-century fiction, both in England and in America.

The need for this study is symbolized by the fact that there is at present no historical term to denote the literary movement which is my subject. My greatest difficulty has been one of terminology. Are these writers "late Romantics," "primitivists," "naturalists," "social realists," "evolutionary utopians"? Each label is useful, but ultimately inadequate and misleading.

Thus I have found it not only convenient but necessary to invent a term for the movement I hope to trace. I have used the word "naturist" not only because it suggests the essential insight of the movement, but also because the term is devoid of established literary connotations. It is the purpose of this study to provide those connotations, and thus to define the word "naturist," not in abstract language, but in terms of the concrete effect of the novels themselves.

It may be helpful at the outset to provide a working definition of the word. The naturist world is a world of physical organism, where biology replaces theology as the source both of psychic health and of moral authority. The naturist is a child of Darwin; he sees man as part of an animal continuum; he reasserts the importance of instinct as a key to human happiness; he tends to be suspicious of the life of the mind; he is wary of abstractions. He is in revolt against Christian dogma, against conventional morality, against the ethic which reigns in a commercial society. His themes are inevitably utopian; his attention is seldom diverted from questions of social organization, and usually some elements of socialism are at work in his philosophy. As a novelist, he is likely to prefer a loose plot structure, built around an elaborately described landscape. As a descriptive artist, he tends to dislike the fixity of the still photograph, and he anticipates, in many respects, the effect of the "moving" pictures which are coming to birth during these same years. Finally, he is part of that larger movement on behalf of sexual liberation which is one of the marks of English literature from 1890 to our own day.

These writers comprise a loosely knit family: the naturist spectrum extends from the relatively primitivist group (Hudson, Tomlinson, perhaps D. H. Lawrence) to the liberal humanist group represented by Butler and Forster.

I am indebted to Dan Laurence for advice and encouragement, and to Anthony Billings for invaluable help in preparing the manuscript.

1 Hardy: A Better World

It is now a good many years since Husserl set forth the motto,
"Zu den Sachen selbst," "to the things themselves," as an exhortation to philosophers to bring themselves closer to the
sources of experience. To do so is very hard for philosophers:
they come to experience with too many intellectual preconcep-
tions. Artists are better at it.

William Barrett, Irrational Man

It might be said that the twentieth-century philosopher has set himself the task of presenting reality rather than analysing it. Bergson's
"duration," Whitehead's "event," Dewey's "mind," Camus' "absurd,"
Heidegger's "existence" – each formulation points to a dimension
of experience beneath the grasp of clear and distinct ideas. Husserl's
"things themselves" are individual entities, and as such are ultimately incomprehensible. For this task of presenting concrete experience, the artist is surely better equipped than the philosopher; thus
Santayana, Sartre, and Camus take to writing novels; Dostoievsky
and Kafka are glossed by theologians; Nietzsche, Sartre, and Whitehead become literary critics; Conrad and Hardy are discovered to be
proto-existentialists; and B. J. Lonergan, a respected Jesuit theo-
logian, can assert that "the artists have become the true moralists
of the age."

Nowhere in fiction is this quality of concreteness better exemplified
than in the novels of Thomas Hardy. The topography of Wessex, its
vegetation, its insect and animal life, and the physical attitudes of
its human inhabitants, are the raw material of Hardy's fiction. His
growth as a novelist is directly related to his increasing ability to
push beyond "word-painting" – the tableau effect of *Two on a Tower*
– and to develop the immediate and tactile quality of description that
gives such irreducible solidity to Egdon Heath, or Tess's dairy farm,
or Jude's Christminster. D. H. Lawrence admired Hardy for his
"sensuous understanding . . . deeper than that, perhaps, of any other

English novelist";[1] and Joseph Warren Beach writes of "Mr. Hardy's extreme fondness for facts," and adds that "there is something touching about the way he leans upon them, his naive faith that in them salvation is to be found."[2]

It is only in the careful description of concrete fact that Hardy can embrace the paradox, the abiding dilemma that lies, like Egdon, beneath civilization. "A novel," wrote Hardy, "is an impression, not an argument."[3] Perhaps too much attention has been given to Hardy's ideas, his "philosophy." Hardy's truth is his quality of vision; it is the style and texture of his novels. His importance for the writers who follow him – and for twentieth-century fiction in general – rests upon the impression his novels give, not upon his attitudes, opinions, or ideas. For Hardy seemed to be saying, with Yeats: "Man can embody truth but he cannot know it."[4]

In Hardy's novels man's body seems to grow, like a tree, from the soil. Farmer Gabriel Oak, in *Far From the Madding Crowd*, is deeply rooted in the soil from which he derives his sustenance, his name, and his sturdy character. Bathhsheba, Fanny, Troy, Boldwood – all move around the monumental figure of Oak and the land he symbolizes.

If man is part of the landscape in *Madding Crowd*, Hardy's landscape is itself humanized in *The Return of the Native*. Egdon Heath is presented to the reader, in the first chapter heading, as "A Face on Which Time Makes but Litttle Impression." Egdon seems to "wake and listen," and to feel at last the human emotion of love: "The storm was its lover, and the wind its friend" (5). These first pages of the novel quickly identify Egdon Heath as "a place perfectly accordant with man's nature – neither ghastly, hateful, nor ugly; neither commonplace, unmeaning, nor tame; but like man, slighted and enduring" (6).

The humanizing of Egdon Heath is more than a convenient metaphor: it is the very soul of the novel, the source of both character and plot. The "lonely face" of Egdon suggests the "tragic possibilities" that will become actual in the plot. But the metaphoric face of Egdon is only a prelude; as the novel progresses, metaphor yields to direct description of the organic life which springs from the heath. In his last novels, *Tess of the d'Urbervilles* and *Jude the Obscure*, Hardy discards metaphor: his landscape becomes literal and stark, as if to suggest that the traditional device of metaphor has become inadequate for his purposes, creating, as it does, too wide a poetic distance between the thing itself and the writer's sensibility. We are made to feel Tess's physical movement across the land from the beginning of the story until her final moments at Stonehenge, and in her movement is her story. *Jude* begins with a vivid sense of concreteness, especially in the scenes between Jude and Arabella. But one of the themes of the book is modern man's loss of contact with the physical world, and in the latter portions of the novel, Hardy's style reflects this sense of estrangement and abstraction. Yet the novel is structured around an elaborate symbolism of location, as the chapter headings suggest ("At Marygreen," "At Christminster," "At Melchester," etc.). From the detailed map of Wessex, which first appeared at the front of *Madding Crowd*, Hardy moves toward that sensuous immediacy of landscape characteristic of the later novels. The naturists inherit this exuberant awareness of the earth from Hardy. Hudson, Tomlinson, Douglas, Forster, and Lawrence continually suspend the action of their characters to study the shape and contours of the landscape on which they move.

It can hardly be claimed that Hardy and the naturists were responsible for this renewed attention to landscape and the world of nature in modern English literature. Clearly such credit belongs to their forbears, the Romantic poets, and especially to the poems of Wordsworth. The naturists are deeply indebted to the Romantic movement in matters of style as well as theme. But were the naturists in fact merely translating Wordsworthian nature-worship from poetry into fiction, or did their inspiration have a more immediate and independent origin? Surely they shared with the Romantics an interest in the "unknown modes of being" associated with the world of physical nature. But Wordsworth's response to nature is located still within the epistemological world of John Locke: from the contemplation of a natural setting, Wordsworth derives ideas and feelings. His intimations of immortality end with "soothing thoughts," "the philosophic mind," and "thoughts that do often lie too deep for tears."

The naturists, on the contrary, are closer to the unconscious-centered psychology of Freud, Jung, and William James than to the empirical psychology of John Locke; they are suspicious of any conversion of landscape into philosophy, and reject the idea of an empirical event in nature as an occasion for abstract or general thought. Lawrence finds a truth in Hardy's novels "greater than ever the human mind can grasp," and seeks to evoke the same intuitive awareness in his own novels. Virginia Woolf has a similar reaction to Hardy's novels: ". . . there is always about them a little blur of un-

consciousness, that halo of freshness and margin of the unexpressed."[5]
This "margin of the unexpressed" is of course present in Wordsworth's poems as it is in all good poetry; but in the naturist novel it
is central, not marginal. E. M. Forster was alluding to this fact when
he wrote of Shakespeare and the Romantics as being "subconsciously
aware of the subconscious," in contrast to modern novelists, who
"have conscious knowledge of it."[6]

Wordsworth's poetic vision presumes a distance between the object
(the landscape) and the subject (the poet). The naturist tendency,
culminating in Lawrence, is to avoid this subject–object separation
by closing the personal subject within the impersonal world of nature.
Thus the naturist is post-Romantic in his attempt to obliterate the
observing, thinking, feeling first-person, the Wordsworthian "I." This
naturist impulse anticipates the techniques later developed by Pound,
Eliot, and Joyce, to alter the personal lyric voice into the dramatic
voice of a *persona*, placed within a larger objective framework. To the
later writers, that framework is aesthetic and mythic; for the naturist,
it is natural and ontological. His characters, like the tiny figures in
the immense spaces of a Chinese screen painting, or like the grass-
hopper-sized Clym Yeobright cutting furze, are themselves part of the
landscape. Lawrence's exhortation, "just be oneself, like a walking
flower," though it would be quickly understood by a student of Zen
or the Tao, would likely have seemed absurd to Wordsworth, Shelley,
or Tennyson.

The naturist rejects all ideals, including the Romantic ideal of
nature. When Lawrence shudders at Shelley's lines, "Hail to thee,
blithe Spirit! / Bird thou never wert," he was rather heartlessly
articulating this naturist aversion to the spiritualizing and idealizing
of natural phenomena. Where Wordsworth seeks to assimilate meaning out of nature into mind, Lawrence reverses direction, allowing
nature to draw back into itself the contingent mind: ". . . the mind
has no existence by itself, it is only the glitter of the sun on the surface of the waters."[7] Wordsworth might have accepted this statement
as an apt metaphor; but for Lawrence it is not metaphor. He means it
literally. In the same way, Hardy's personification of Egdon Heath is
misunderstood if it is taken as an example of the Pathetic Fallacy. He
is referring to an actual wisdom literally present in nature, though
unfathomable to the mind of man. This sea-change in the traditional
use of metaphor signals a radical redefinition of the place of human
beings in the world of nature; and it is this new and quite original
view of nature which identifies and distinguishes naturism as a de-

parture within the larger context of the Romantic movement of the
nineteenth century.

What was responsible for the change? In a word, it was the vision
of Charles Darwin, penetrating to the process beneath the appearance. Darwin's *The Voyage of the Beagle* was the platform upon which
naturism was built. Indeed, for the novelist at the end of the nineteenth century, if there had been no Charles Darwin, he would have
to have been invented. From Flaubert and Balzac to Zola, from the
Brontës and Jane Austen to Dickens and George Eliot, the basic
critique of industrial and bourgeois life had been made. The vein had
been thoroughly explored, and it was difficult to see how any new
novelist could do it better. The miseries and inequities and snobberies
and hypocrisies had been exposed; yet within this great tradition
of realism in the novel, there were few premonitions of new possibilities or constructive alternatives for the individual or for bourgeois
society. The utopian spirit of the humanists More and Erasmus – a
spirit which was, in fact, sanely pragmatic – was conspicuously absent
from the nineteenth-century novel, which set itself only the indispensable task of reporting things as they were.

To be sure, Marxism and the various streams of socialism and
anarchism were steadily gaining hold among intellectuals, and the
spirit of the French Revolution was far from dormant within the
working class; but for the time, these movements remained under-
currents of theory, seminal but still powerless. In England, Ruskin's
criticism of industrialism was accurate and telling, but his own vision
of an alternative society, like that of William Morris, seemed contrived, artificial, and distant from the consciousness of the ordinary
man. What was needed was a utopia after the manner of More,
Erasmus, and Rabelais – a utopia founded upon a *donnée*, a given truth
already present ontologically in nature and not contrived by the
theory-ridden minds of men. A new generation of novelists sought to
build upon the nineteenth-century critique of bourgeois society in a
constructive way, by seeking out a new (though very old) authority,
the authority of human and physical nature. The naturist novel was
built, not upon a new set of ideals, but upon a new quality of vision
which first appeared in the works of Charles Darwin.

It is characteristic of any scientific discovery that phenomena which
had previously seemed uninteresting and unexceptional suddenly
become fascinating and resonant with meaning. The microscopic
quality of Darwin's vision meant that an arid plain became for the
first time as interesting as a florid life-filled jungle. A favorite province

of naturist description is the desolate landscape – Hardy's "gaunt waste in Thule," Butler's bare Alpine entrance to Erewhon, Douglas's Calabria, Forster's Marabar, Doughty's vast Arabian deserts. Darwin had introduced this central naturist theme on the first page of *The Voyage of the Beagle*: "The neighborhood of Porto Praya, viewed from the sea, wears a desolate aspect. . . . The island would generally be considered as uninteresting; but to any one accustomed only to an English landscape, the novel aspect of an utterly sterile land possesses a grandeur which more vegetation might spoil."[8]

Darwin's writing provided a basis for the naturists to hope that modern man could find a way out of the prison of bourgeois institutions to a better world. Darwin's promise of amelioration is framed in the slower rhythms of biological rather than human time, but it was interpreted by the naturists to be as sure as evolution itself: ". . . and the fact of his having thus risen," Darwin wrote, "instead of having been aboriginally placed there, may give him hope for a still higher destiny in the distant future."[9] The naturists recognized that this "still higher destiny" would emerge, not from the schemes and theories of men – not from Hobbes, Locke, Rousseau, or Marx – but from the quieter and more enduring geological truth hidden within Egdon Heath, the Marabar Caves, the Arabian deserts, and the Amazonian jungles. Thus in Hardy's "The Darkling Thrush," it is no human prophet, but rather the "ecstatic sound" of bird-song which offers the dejected poet "Some blessed Hope, whereof he knew / And I was unaware." This song of hope echoes throughout naturist literature, and distinguishes it from both the nineteenth-century realist novel and the twentieth-century novel of existential despair.

Throughout *The Voyage of the Beagle* Darwin sensed, even before he understood, that the genius of nature lay in its capacity to create variety. Any general theory in science is an attempt to grasp the single principle of operation which explains the widest possible group of events. But Darwin's extraordinary achievement was to discover that the simplest principle of biological process was the principle of proliferation itself: in its variety was its simplicity, for selection was contingent upon mutation. Organisms survive by means of genetic mutations which are random, accidental, irrational and unpredictable in any individual; it is the environment which selects the mutations and thus provides the principle of unity. This sense of a random and accidental process, operating in terms of unknowable specifics but always within a larger and purposeful plan, marks the uniqueness of Darwin's discoveries in the history of science: nature becomes historical and triumphs over history's accidents. But this triumph has nothing to do with the human mind or human thought; it is the environment, not the mind of man, which provides the principle of unity, the plan, and the wisdom to survive. "Natural selection," wrote Darwin, "is a power incessantly ready for action, and is as immeasurably superior to man's feeble efforts, as the works of Nature are to those of Art."[10] "How fleeting are the wishes of man! how short his time! and consequently how poor will be his results, compared with those accumulated by Nature during whole geological periods! "[11]

The naturists caught from Darwin this central recognition: that the rich profusion of nature contained an adaptive principle far superior to any ideas that might be fabricated by the human mind. The principle of natural selection can be known, but its operation in any particular instance cannot; knowledge of the principle of evolution provides specific data about the past, but not about the future. "Thought is abstract," cries Heard in *South Wind*; had he not abhorred syllogism, he might have added that abstraction is reduction, and that to reduce is to falsify. The naturists insist, with Darwin, that the thought is not the thing. At the end of the naturist adventure, in 1922, the philosopher Alfred North Whitehead would call this superstitious attribution of truth to abstract concepts "the Fallacy of Misplaced Concreteness."

The naturists are not anti-intellectual, for they recognize the indispensable but limited function of human thought for the preservation of the species *homo sapiens*. Unlike other animals, humans must know in order to survive; but the content of knowledge necessary to human well-being is small. America's early naturist, Thoreau, suggests as much in *Walden*: "Rescue the drowning and tie your shoe-strings." But when knowledge proliferates, as it has in our civilization, far beyond its limited function, it becomes, as it did in Eden, the cause of our fall. The naturist novel returns always to Eden, where there is no knowledge, only wisdom: Clym to Egdon, Tess to Stonhenge, Abel to Patagonia, Stephen to Cadbury Rings, Heard to Nepenthe, Tomlinson's narrator to his Amazonian garden, Birkin and Ursula to Sherwood Forest. It is Birkin who, at the very end of *Women in Love*, best expresses the central naturist inheritance from Darwin: "Whatever the mystery which has brought forth man and the universe, it is a non-human mystery, it has its own great ends, man is not the criterion."

Darwin's admiration for what he calls "profitable variations" in nature is in part responsible for a renewed respect among the naturists for individual differences. "Under the term of 'variations,' " Darwin wrote, "it must never be forgotten that mere individual differences are included."[12] In the scheme of evolution, a genetic characteristic which is dormant and maladapted in one kind of environment may become crucial to survival in another. Transforming biology into sociology (as he often did), the naturist sensed that the tendency of any society to ostracize or punish the non-conformist hinders the evolution of the species. The survival of the fittest is thus contingent upon the survival of the misfit. The naturist novel is populated with characters, from Ernest Pontifex and Jude Fawley through Stephen Wonham and Aaron Sisson, who are outcasts, rogues, idlers, eccentrics, drunkards, bi-sexuals, adulteresses – in short, barbarians. After all, Charles Darwin himself had noticed that "there can hardly be a doubt that we are descended from barbarians."[13]

Finally, it was Darwin's use of language in *The Voyage of the Beagle* that furnished a pattern for the prose style of the naturist travel book and novel. The rhythms and periods of Darwin's prose constitute a unique style, a blend of minute observation and interpretative comment. Darwin's language communicates a quiet but constant thrill of discovery, a controlled excitement at his encounter with a hitherto lost world. His nature description possesses a luminous quality which projects, beneath its literal surface, a sense of wonder at this discovery of a brave new world that has such creatures in it. For a poetic equivalent, one thinks of the radiant crescendo of Dante's verse in the "Paradiso" cantos. Such a comparison is not as absurd as it might appear: Darwin's world was prosaic and material, Dante's exalted and incorporeal; Dante looked up, to the unfolding celestial rose, Darwin looked down, to the unfolding fronds of Tahiti. But each is encountering what for him is a literal truth, each is finding an Eden which had been lost but now is a living presence, uncovered to the senses and the intelligence. In both works, the governing metaphor is the physical image of light. And for the generation of naturists who followed Darwin, this newly discerned paradise appeared as wonderful and hallowed as Dante's was to his readers. If Dante's rose was mystical, so too was the naturist landscape. Butler's exalted vision of an Alpine promontory is akin to the humiliating revelation of Adela's real self in the Marabar Caves. The naturist, in short, experienced a religious awe no less intense than that of Dante.

In the first two decades of the twentieth century, landscape becomes a dominating presence in English fiction. Darwin's influence –

and in turn, Hardy's – can be measured, not only in terms of the new importance of landscape description, but more significantly in terms of the new manner in which landscape enters the art of story-telling.

Landscape in the Renaissance pastoral romance of Poliziano or Tasso, Spenser or Sidney, was deliberately enamelled and two-dimensional. Surface color and design provided a static frame, a background for the conventionalized action of the protagonists. Renaissance pastoral poets were not interested in recapturing the vivid concreteness, the tangibility, of Dante's "Inferno" or "Purgatorio," or of Chaucer's *Canterbury Tales*. But in Hardy's "pastoral tragedy" landscape comes alive. No longer a backdrop, it becomes, to use Aldous Huxley's phrase about Lawrence, a "principal personage" whose presence is felt in terms of a new sensuous grasp of space. For Hardy himself seems to be impatient with the secondary qualities of things; he seeks the enduring monumental shape which lies beneath the distortions and limited perspectives of human vision.

Hardy's point of view as novelist is in the tradition of the omniscient narrator; his vision is often Olympian and panoramic; he sees landscape from above, as one looks at a map. Lawrence noticed that at times "the map appears to us more real than the land" ("Study," 420), and Auden spoke of Hardy's "hawk's vision."[14] It is characteristic of Hardy that the title he first chose for *The Dynasts* was "A Bird's-Eye View of Europe at the Beginning of the Nineteenth Century."

This sense of the spatial distance of the narrator from the action is essential to the pathos – or the tragic irony – of Hardy's novels. At times, in fact, Hardy seems to be looking at his characters through a telescope. The title "Two on a Tower" conveys an effect of telescopic distance which so often frames his novels, locates the action at every moment, and embraces the contradictions so essential to Hardy's mood. The beginnings of *The Mayor of Casterbridge* and *The Return of the Native*, and the ending of *Tess of the d'Urbervilles*, all have a quality of universality which is projected by means of a sense of visual distance.

Hardy's "bird's-eye view," his "hawk-like vision," was the last of its kind in English literature. In a world grown vastly more complex and unmanageable, a world where "things fall apart," few novelists would again have the temerity to try to put things together again through the integrating vision of an omniscient narrator. The twentieth-century novelist would attempt to solve the problem by means of an imposition of myth upon chaos; yet the immediate data of literature would become increasingly more subjective, until in Joyce's Molly Bloom a whole cosmos would seem to center upon a kind of organic purring, a physical vibration emanating from heart, stomach, and womb.

Yet this very imagery of teeming life within the organism has its beginning in Hardy; for when he wishes to convey the intensity, movement, and change of the organic life which springs from his landscape, he is equally capable of an opposite, a microscopic, distortion. It is as though Hardy were trying to move from the eighteenth-century Newtonian world of vast spaces to a nineteenth-century world of biological scrutiny. Hardy signals, in the age of Darwin, the advent of a new novelistic language: the language of organic change, of germination and growth. His visual imagination is profoundly affected by the new enthusiasm for the microscope: "I sit under a tree, and feel alone: I think of certain insects around me as magnified by the microscope; creatures like elephants, flying dragons, etc. And I feel I am by no means alone."[15] Just as telescopic distance reduces Hardy's humans to ant-size, so through the intercession of the microscopic lens, the smallest insect takes on a relevance of human proportions.

The diary notation quoted above was written in 1875, and it anticipates the entomological imagery of *Return*, published in 1879. Clym Yeobright's daily life was "of a curious microscopic sort"; "bees hummed," "butterflies alighted," and

> tribes of emerald-green grasshoppers leaped over his feet, falling awkwardly on their backs, heads or hips, like unskilful acrobats, as chance might rule: or engaged themselves in noisy flirtations under the fern-fronds with silent ones of homely hue. Huge flies, ignorant of larders and wire-netting, and quite in a savage state, buzzed about him without knowing that he was a man. (298)

And in answer Clym sings, in the tradition of Colin Clout, a hymn to nature:

> "L'oiseau réprend doux chant d'amour
> Tout célèbre dans la nature
> Le point de jour." (299)

Clym's joy as part of the insect and animal world is only a prelude to the almost myopic intensity of Mrs. Yeobright's vision a few pages later. As she sets out toward Alderworth, she penetrates much further than Clym into the dark origins of Darwin's species:

Occasionally she came to a spot where independent worlds of ephemerons were passing their time in mad carousal, some in the tepid and stringy water of a nearly dried pool. All the shallower ponds had decreased to a vaporous mud amid which the maggoty shapes of innumerable obscure creatures could be indistinctly seen, heaving and wallowing with enjoyment. (327)

In this passage the human metaphor is still present, but is carefully blended with a concrete impression of the orgiastic movement within the lower organic world. Mrs. Yeobright senses that the "maggoty shapes of innumerable obscure creatures" are far more real than her "indistinct" vision can ever indicate. Hardy has here dispensed with the traditional devices of landscape description: the picture is "vaporous" and "obscure"; but the "maggoty shapes" take on a plastic reality which transcends imagery, a concreteness more immediate than if they were merely "seen." This is a quality of nature description that will not be found before the age of Darwin. It is a kind of language which will separate Hardy, along with the naturist writers who develop and refine his technique, from the quality of description in such novels as *Wuthering Heights* or *The Heart of Midlothian*, or such a poem as *The Prelude*. Hardy's careful combination of metaphor and organic image has opened up a new dimension of physical reality for twentieth-century fiction: the microscopic world of man's origins, the teeming locale of the evolutionary roots of human existence. This microscopic examination of the vegetable and insect world will dominate such novels as *Green Mansions, Sons and Lovers,* and *The Rainbow,* and such travel books as *Idle Days in Patagonia* or *The Sea and the Jungle.* This new imagery will have a special relevance to the emotional life of man: Havelock Ellis, in his discussions of sexuality, will speak of human beings as "we metazoa,"[16] and Ellis, Edward Carpenter, and Norman Douglas will begin their studies in sexual selection by examining, and carefully describing, the process of parthenogenesis.

When finally her son Clym is pointed out to her, "Mrs. Yeobright strained her eyes. . . . He appeared of a russet hue, not more distinguishable from the scene around him than the green caterpillar from the leaf it feeds on" (328). Throughout this section of *Return,* Hardy seems to strain, along with Mrs. Yeobright, in order to see more deeply into the yeasty orgy of microscopic life from which all higher forms, including man, have emerged. What Hardy sees there is indeed an orgy: he sees joy.

Yet in the novels of Hardy, the most sustained and ecstatic passages of botanical description come as preludes to tragedy. Mrs. Yeobright's vision of the luxuriant beauty of Clym's garden immediately precedes her being turned away from his closed door, to die from the sting of an adder. This adder-snake, and the apple tree Mrs. Yeobright sees in Clym's green dooryard, are suggestions of Eden; her fall occurs in a garden setting of happiness-in-nature which, though lost, is not irretrievable to man. It is this unachieved but real possibility of happiness, suggested by Hardy's manner of description, which makes the passage so moving.

Hardy's originality in dealing with landscape involves not only a new manner of description, but also a new way of relating landscape and the organic life upon it to his characters. Each novel seems to focus upon some form of organic life in terms of which the characters themselves are described. Clym is of the insect world, "a mere parasite of the heath, fretting its surface in his daily labour as a moth frets a garment" (328). Clym and Eustacia are seen as "two horns which the sluggish heath had put forth from its crown like a mollusc, and had now again drawn in" (328). The opening chapters of *Jude* center upon his experiences with animals: Jude's job as scarecrow (11), where he identifies with the birds; the episode of the pig's pizzle (41), and, later, the trauma he undergoes helping Arabella slaughter a pig (73). Tess's first guilt is over the death of a horse (32); she is given a job whistling to bullfinches (70), then one milking cows (138); she is seen as a fly (136), then as a sparrow (168); she feels compassion for pheasants which have been shot and are dying (354); she watches strange "nameless birds" (367) migrating from the North Pole; she is herself "like a bird caught in a springe clap-net" (370); and as she dies, "her breathing now was quick and small, like that of a lesser creature than a woman" (505).

Hardy's diaries indicate that he was extraordinarily fond of animals, and his empathy extends to the vegetable world as well. In *The Woodlanders*, for example, the foliage and fruit of forest and orchard occupy the center of Hardy's world. Havelock Ellis, as early as 1883, noticed that "Mr. Hardy is never more reverent, more exact, than when he is speaking of forest trees."[17] D. H. Lawrence was speaking Hardy-language when he wrote, in 1922: "I would like to be a tree for a while";[18] but it was Hardy himself, in 1877, who expressed the real reason for his reverence: "I sometimes look upon all things in inanimate nature as pensive mutes" (*Life*, 114).

Hardy's method of describing landscape reflects this sense of all things in nature as "pensive mutes," and this quality in his fiction will be echoed continually in the travel literature and fiction of the naturists. Hudson's tropical birds and Patagonian wastes, Tomlinson's Amazonian flora, Douglas's sun-baked sirocco, Forster's wych-elm, Lawrence's vibrant flowers – all will have "mute" voices, and will speak a yet-undeciphered language of wisdom.

Is Hardy's statement merely poetic metaphor, a tame echo of the "still, sad music of humanity" which Wordsworth heard in the world of physical nature? In Hardy's generation the poetic device of personification had acquired a scientific justification which had been absent in the age of Wordsworth. Darwin and his English disciple Thomas Henry Huxley had broken down the traditional discrete divisions within the "chain of being"; they had provided a new continuity and a new basis – physical, rather than theological – for perceiving and expressing the relationship between man and lower forms of nature. Huxley states the matter at issue succinctly in a passage that is quoted and glossed, in turn, by Hardy's friend Edward Clodd, in his book on Huxley: "The attempt to draw a psychical distinction between man and beast is futile, and . . . even the highest faculties of feeling and of intellect begin to germinate in lower forms of life."[19]

This doctrine is helpful in understanding Hardy's attribution of a kind of intelligence to vegetable and animal life. "The highest faculties of feeling and intellect" must express a "meaning," and "meaning" implies a mode of expression, a form of language. If Hardy and the naturists depart from Huxley's basic meaning, it is in ascribing to lower forms of life a wisdom higher than civilized man's, a lost language of Eden before the fall. In *The Woodlanders*, this "alphabet" is expressed in terms of clear physical sensations:

. . . those remoter signs and symbols which, seen in few, were of runic obscurity, but all together made an alphabet. From the light lashing of the twigs upon their faces, when brushing through them in the dark, they could pronounce upon the species of the tree whence they stretched; from the quality of the wind's murmur through a bough they could in like manner name its sort afar off. (399)

Earlier, in *Return*, night sounds on Egdon become a catalyst for human sounds; yet the purposely obscure wording of the passage makes it unclear whether Eustacia's "articulation" takes the form of human speech or not. Her "discourse" mingles strangely, and becomes identified, with the "wild rhetoric of night":

> Suddenly, on the barrow, there mingled with all this wild rhetoric of night a sound which modulated so naturally with the rest that its beginning and ending were hardly to be distinguished. The bluffs, and the bushes, and the heather-bells had broken silence; at last, so did the woman; and her articulation was but as another phrase of the same discourse as theirs. (61)

Still earlier – and no doubt when Huxley's influence was strongest – in *Madding Crowd*, Hardy's humans haltingly learn, like children, a new language: "The instinctive act of humankind was to stand and listen, and learn how the trees on the right and the trees on the left wailed or chaunted to each other in the regular antiphonies of a cathedral choir . . ." (9). Again, the "wild rhetoric" of nature begets a human reply. As the plaintive chant comes to an end, a new sound is heard, an antiphon not of nature, but not of human discourse either: "Suddenly an unexpected series of sounds began to be heard in this place up against the sky. They had a clearness which was to be found nowhere in the wind, and a sequence which was to be found nowhere in nature. They were the notes of Farmer Oak's flute" (10). It is precisely this kind of antiphon, which, a generation later, will be a central preoccupation in the poetry of Wallace Stevens.

Farmer Oak's flute marks the beginning of a symbolism of the individual melodic voice which became one of the dominating images of naturist literature. "Life," for Samuel Butler's Overton, "is like a fugue";[20] and Butler's addiction to Handel, along with Hardy's imagery of music, was echoed in the music-symbolism of Hudson, Forster, Tomlinson, and Lawrence. Oak's flute is one of several symbols used by Hardy to point to a world that lies beneath rationality. "My own interest," he wrote, "lies largely in non-rationalistic subjects, since non-rationality seems, so far as one can perceive, to be the principle of the Universe . . . lying at the indifference point between rationality and irrationality" (*Life*, 309). This remark aptly describes the effect of Hardy's nature imagery. Farmer Oak's flute and the many "voices" which resound in Hardy's world of nature represent the search for a new vocabulary to describe the interior life of man. In Hardy, man's unconscious life is anchored immediately and constantly in physical nature – not only in man's own animality, but in the whole external world of organic life. Hardy's "alphabet" is a language of spiritualized physiognomy, physiology, botany, and topography. The next generation of novelists will be deeply indebted to Hardy for pointing the way toward a new novelistic language to express the unconscious life of man.

Hardy's plots evolve from a continual interplay between self-conscious voluntary action, on the one hand, and incomprehensible passive suffering, on the other. The force that puts Tess on the road to Alec d'Urberville is her mother's willfulness; Tess herself remains compliant and receptive throughout the story; even her death she accepts with pathetic gratitude. It is Eustacia's strength of will which destroys her; but Clym's purpose in returning to Egdon is to abandon the constant acquisitive pressure required by the diamond trade, in order to bind himself again to the soil of Egdon. Sue Bridehead's willfulness may be capricious, contradictory, and neurotic; but it is always on the mark, insuperable, and deadly. Jude's determination to learn is itself the instrument of his destruction in the closed world of Christminster. Willfulness for Hardy is the epitome of disembodied consciousness; it springs from self-delusion and ends in self-destruction. Only the passive characters, in these novels, are wise. Hardy's historical poem *The Dynasts* is the most striking expression of his belief that "no man is a rationalist, and that human actions are not ruled by reason at all in the last resort" (*Life*, 403). Napoleon symbolizes, in *The Dynasts*, the illusory victory of the willful individual over "passive" history. Hardy conceives his "epic" as "a spectral force seen acting in a man (Napoleon) and he acting under it – a pathetic sight – this compulsion" (*Life*, 416).

"This compulsion" – this powerful illusion of unfettered free will – is the primary source of tragedy in Hardy's fiction: this is Hardy's hubris. Long before *The Dynasts* was written, Hardy had clearly fixed its theme: "Action mostly automatic; reflex movements, etc. Not the result of what is called *motive*, though always ostensibly so, even to the actor's own consciousness" (*Life*, 148). This "spectral force" is the authentically effective power in human affairs. It operates, not through human acts of will, but through receptivity and acquiescence. Historical events and tendencies are "in the main the outcome of *passivity* – acted upon by unconscious propensity" (*Life*, 168). For Hardy, passivity is a state of sanity and health, in that it allows a clear channel for the expression of the "unconscious propensity" which underlies rational "motive." Years later William James will discover, in his investigation of the place of the unconscious in religious experience, that nervous disorders are often cleared by a relaxation of voluntary effort. James found that self-realization could

be "*jammed*, as it were, like the lost word when we seek too ener-
getically to recall it." He adds: "Where . . . the subconscious forces
take the lead, it is more probably the better self *in posse* which
directs the operation."[21] James and Hardy are asserting that the
normative pattern for psychic health is to be found in the realm of
biological organism rather than in the province of conceptual
morality.

This insight lies at the heart of naturist literature. The naturist interest in actions which are "not the result of what is called *motive*"
ultimately brought about a revolution in plot structure, for the new
novelists converted Hardy's doubt about "motive" into a new literary form. Their determination to allow "subconscious forces to take
the lead" resulted in plots built, not upon Hardy's coincidental event,
but upon an apparently unmotivated character action analogous to
Gide's "acte gratuit." And James's concept of the "better self *in
posse*" became the prevailing theme of the novels of Hudson, Forster,
Douglas, Wells, and Lawrence. There are two sides to any artistic
coin; the naturists reversed the coin of Hardy's pastoral tragedy and
found, on the other side, a new kind of pastoral myth.

The pastoral genre, ancient and modern, has always concealed
beneath its placid surface highly charged comments on political and
social issues. Hardy's use of pastoral settings and themes expresses his
sense of the opposition between man in nature and man in society.
Increasingly Hardy tended to see an opposition between the spontaneity of nature and the legal rigidities of social institutions and
conventions. The premonitions of social criticism in his earlier novels
became explicit and impassioned in *Tess* and *Jude*. The experience
of Tess, for example, which involved a biting criticism of the role of
woman as "sexual property," had been prefigured by the tragedy
of Fanny Robin in *Madding Crowd*. In the earlier novels the theme of
marriage-tyranny was employed primarily as an effective device for
story pathos: in *Madding Crowd*, Bathsheba's impulsive marriage to
Sergeant Troy is suddenly terminated, with all the arbitrariness of an
omnipotent author, by the murder of Troy, and the way is
cleared for a happy liaison between Bathsheba and Oak. Skepticism
about marriage as a legal institution was implicit in *The Mayor of
Casterbridge* and *The Return of the Native*. But Hardy's caustic view
of marriage lay boldly and explicitly on the surface of *Tess* and *Jude*.

This development, which occurred between *The Woodlanders*
(1889) and *Tess* (1893), reflected a general renewal of social consciousness in England during the 1880s and 1890s. The legalization

of the trade unions in 1871 and 1876, the birth of the Fabian Society in 1883, the mob uprisings of 1886, the "Bloody Sunday" riots of 1887, the London Dock Strike of 1889; the indictment of Vizetelly, in 1888, for publishing the novels of Zola; the coming-to-age of a new generation of working people educated by the Act of 1870 – all these events contributed to a social awakening. Ibsen had appeared on the English scene: translations by Gosse, Jones, and Archer began to appear in 1876. The famous 1889 production of *A Doll's House*, the suppression of *Ghosts* in 1891, and Shaw's powerful essay on Ibsen (1891), contributed to the change in Hardy which first becomes clearly evident in *Tess of the d'Urbervilles*. By 1890, Hardy's notebooks and conversation betray an intense interest in the plays of Ibsen. In any event, "the claims of the ideal," Ibsen's term for a hypocritical bourgeois morality, assume a vastly more important place in Hardy's last two novels. The distinctions had always been present: in *Return*, for example, Hardy's attractive description of pagan customs which had "survived medieval doctrine" (459) might be taken as a veiled comment on Christianity; but such a judgement is left wholly to the reader. In *Tess* Hardy leaves no doubt; his point of view emerges both in dialogue and in the author's voice, and in either case tends to be clumsily latinate and abstract. Thus Hardy describes Tess, with more truth than beauty: "Most of her misery had been generated by her conventional aspect, and not by her innate sensations" (115).

"The question of the day," wrote Samuel Butler in *The Way of All Flesh*, "is marriage and the family system" (337). Hardy's *Tess* (1893), Shaw's *Mrs. Warren's Profession* (1894), and George Moore's *Esther Waters* (1894), continue Ibsen's attack upon the legal bondage of woman. In *Tess*, Hardy approaches the questions of marriage and family with a new intensity achieved through a sharper and more sustained insight into the inner life of his characters. If conventional attitudes destroy Tess, she herself is conventional and conformist. Her sense of guilt is the inner reflection, and the ruthless executioner, of a social verdict. But the psychology of conformity is even more striking in the character of Sue Bridehead. Like Tess, Sue is described in the first chapters of *Jude* in terms of her attractive natural vitality. It is because of this vitality that Sue is destroyed; yet the repressive morality which drains this vitality is an authority to which she soon gives obsessive allegiance. Neither Sue nor Tess is a symbol of revolt; each is the psychological victim of a guilt-inducing morality.

Jude Fawley, on the other hand, does not capitulate, and it is in his character that Hardy's theme of revolt against social convention finds embodiment. Jude is associated from the beginning of the novel with the life of nature; yet he is also endowed with a naive belief in the sanctity of institutions: the church, the university, the sacrament of marriage; and these institutions mercilessly crush him. The clearest anticipation of Jude in Hardy's fiction is Henchard in *Mayor*; but where Henchard is "tamed," Jude is annihilated.

Joseph Warren Beach has noted that "if nature is sometimes referred to in these books as a cruel step-mother, she more often appears as an enlightened champion against the obscurantism of social convention."[22] Sue states the theme toward the end of the novel: "We said – do you remember? – that we would make a virtue of joy. I said it was Nature's intention, Nature's law and *raison d'être*, that we should be joyful in what instincts she afforded us – instincts which civilization had taken upon itself to thwart. What dreadful things I said!" (409). God seems no longer to be an accomplice in cruelty, for when Sue exclaims, "It is no use fighting against God!" Jude answers – and we seem to hear Hardy's voice –"It is only against man and senseless circumstances" (413).

Yet in Hardy's last novels nature never wins in human affairs: if nature's "stir of germination" moves Tess with passion, it is only a futile prompting toward a fearful destination: "A particularly fine spring came round, and the stir of germination was almost audible in the buds; it moved her, as it moved the wild animals, and made her passionate to go" (126).

Tess moves, throughout the novel, over a series of fields and woods, paths and roads; like all Hardy's leading characters, she is on a continual pilgrimage. For Hardy's landscapes are invariably bisected by a road. The lengthy description of Egdon Heath concludes with the image of a clear white line, cutting across the twilight gloom: it is "an old vicinal way, which branched from the great Western road of the Romans, the Via Iceniana, or Ikenild Street" (*Return*, 7). And the next chapter begins: "Along the road walked an old man" (8).

A human figure moving along a highway: this is the characteristic opening of a Hardy novel. Gabriel Oak, walking, meets Bathsheba Everdene, riding; Henchard, with wife and child, approaches a village on foot; Tess sets out to improve her fortunes; and Jude's schoolmaster, Phillotson, prefigures Jude's own departure for Christminster and scholarly achievement.

Hardy's characters, like Spenser's or Bunyan's, are continually moving across the landscape. The boy Jude indeed has read Bunyan, and is frightened as he runs home alone, "trying not to think of giants, Herne the Hunter, Apollyon lying in wait for Christian . . ." (20). Hardy's pilgrims, unlike Bunyan's or Dante's, never arrive, but they do invariably have a goal. Lawrence defined the goal accurately: "None of the heroes and heroines care very much for money or immediate self-preservation, and all of them are struggling hard to come into being." Hardy's novels, wrote Lawrence, are "about becoming complete, or about the failure to become complete" ("Study," 410).

If the final aim of Hardy's leading characters is "to become complete" their proximate goal is a negative one: they are all seeking to escape – Eustacia from the country, Clym from the city, Jude from the uncultured provinces, Tess from lowly social status, Henchard from a bad marriage. Hardy's "great Western road" is a road out of entrapment, a pilgrimage toward freedom. The highway is a symbol of hope, of aspiration. But Hardy's road-map is a document of irony which calls into question the "aspiring mind" which had dominated English poetry from Marlowe's Faustus to Tennyson's Ulysses, English fiction from Defoe's Moll Flanders to Thackeray's Becky Sharp. Hardy was challenging the "claims of the ideal" through which civilization tames and often destroys the individual. For it was no longer Tennyson's "Nature," but civilization itself which, for Hardy, was "so careless of the single life."[23] Hardy's roads, which his characters hope will lead them to freedom, ultimately become labyrinths. When Forster later describes India as covered with (and choked by) a grill of roads and highways, his metaphor shows his debt to Hardy.

During the next two decades Hardy's "Western road" reappeared continually in the English novel as a symbol of man's "struggle to become complete." From Hardy's ancient *via* branched roads and paths over land and sea which took Butler's Ernest to London; James's Strether, Joyce's Stephen, and Bennett's Sophia to Paris; Forster's Lilia, Douglas's Keith, and Lawrence's Aaron to Italy; Kipling's Kim and Forster's Mrs. Moore to India; Conrad's Jim to Malaya, and Lawrence's Kate to Mexico. Hudson's Abel repeated Angel Clare's voyage to Brazil, to be followed years later by Evelyn Waugh's Tony Last, who disintegrated in the same Amazon country which provided a saving vision for Tomlinson. The sturdy legs which transported Tess and Jude gave way to the conveniences of ships, trains, and automobiles; and Wells's two Ponderevos found perhaps the most rapid transit of all from the lunatic world of Tono-Bungay: a balloon.

Hardy's road eventually took English travellers to every corner of the earth: Hudson and Tomlinson to South America, T. E. Lawrence, Cunningham Graham and Wilfrid Scawen Blunt to Arab lands; D. H. Lawrence to New Mexico and Australia; Forster and Durrell to Alexandria. Like Hardy's Mrs. Yeobright, Gabriel Oak, and Tess Durbeyfield, these modern pilgrims were enthusiastic bird-watchers, cow-milkers, butterfly-chasers, and students of nature in general. More significantly, the new pilgrims, unlike Hardy's, always arrived, for better or worse, at a destination.

Hardy's "old vicinal way" marked a beginning. It can hardly be claimed as a "cause" of travel literature; it is rather the symptom of a new direction in English fiction. For Hardy's novels introduced the *genius loci*, "spirit of place," as the predominant symbol of human experience in the new novel.

Hardy's dominant use of "spirit of place" in his last novels is closely connected with his increasingly bitter criticism of institutional morality; and both technique and theme are, in turn, facets of his preoccupation with a broader philosophical problem: the question of the nature and value of abstract thought. In many respects the Hardy of the 1890s can be seen as a literary culmination of the broad nineteenth-century revolt against the rationalistic tradition represented by Descartes, and by Christian humanism in general. Schopenhauer had asserted the primacy of will over idea; Nietzsche had seen abstract morality as an elaborate rationalization rooted in a life-denying instinct; Ibsen had dramatized the unholy alliance between idealism and greedy complacency. The widespread attack on bourgeois morality was for Hardy inseparable from the larger question of the relationship between the general rule and the particular concrete individual, between logic and fact.

Hardy's awakening interest in this question is evident throughout *Tess* and *Jude*, where it finds a focus in the characterizations of Angel Clare and little Father Time. The name "Angel" itself carries a multiple irony: the angelic intelligence is bodiless, abstract. Angel Clare is described as possessing "a hard logical deposit" (*Tess*, 308); he performs "a curiously unnatural sacrifice of humanity to mysticism" (339); he seems concerned always with "general principles, to the disregard of the particular instance" (434). It is this man of high principle, incorruptible virtue, and strong intelligence, who provides the self-righteous turn of the screw that crushes Tess. Angel's cruel moralizing is echoed in Sue Bridehead's brutal readings of the mind of God after her conversion: "My children

– are dead – and it is right that they should be! I am glad – almost. They were sin-begotten. They were sacrificed to teach me how to live! – their death was the first stage of my purification. That's why they have not died in vain" (*Jude*, 439).

But Hardy's attack upon abstract morality reaches its apotheosis in the murder-suicide of little Father Time. This child represents a growing "universal wish not to live" (*Jude*, 406), the result of centuries of enervating, repressive civilization. The boy's terrible final act comes in direct response to the birth of a new life in Sue's baby. Little Time, prefigured by Tess's "Sorrow," is a product of the neurotic relationship between Jude and Sue. He is a symbol for Hardy of modern man's loss of contact with physical reality. Father Time knows no facts; he knows only abstractions: "Children begin with detail, and learn up to the general; they begin with the contiguous, and gradually comprehend the universal. The boy seemed to have begun with the generals of life, and never to have concerned himself with the particulars" (334). Father Time represents the triumph of abstract morality, unencumbered by particulars, over concrete nature. His father Jude's last stone-work is the re-lettering of the repeated phrase of the Ten Commandments: "Thou shalt not" (361). Sue takes up the theme after the death of her babies: "There is something external to us which says, 'You shan't!' First it said 'You shan't learn!' Then it said, 'You shan't labor!' Now it says, 'You shan't love!'" (407).

The pathetic suicide of Father Time – so often criticized as melodrama – is in fact one of Hardy's supreme inventions, a moment of shocking revelation. It strikes a chord which will resound through the fiction of the following decades. Mann's young Hanno Buddenbrooks, end of a bourgeois family line, withers and dies as a child of a like illness, as does Hesse's Hans Giebenrath, in *Beneath the Wheel*. The unlikely offspring of Lilia and Gino will be thrown to his death from a carriage in Forster's first novel, titled – aptly enough – *Where Angels Fear to Tread*.

The creation of Father Time marks a turning-point in the English novel: he symbolizes both an end and a beginning. Born an old man, he represents the death of the special sensual joy of childhood. The attempt to recapture this simple bodily delight was a central preoccupation in the writing of the naturists; for they, like Hardy, were attempting to re-establish contact with the physical earth and the physical body. If twentieth-century fiction has been concerned with a search for the sensual intensity of childhood, then the death of

Father Time is an appropriate symbolic prelude to this rebirth. Proust, Joyce, Mann, Hesse, Hemingway, Fitzgerald, Salinger – all have tried, each in his own way, to take the age out of Father Time.

This sorrowful child also serves to introduce another naturist theme, one which is stated most succinctly (and urbanely) by Keith, in Douglas's *South Wind*: "All morality is a generalization," pontificates Keith in a magnificent generalization, "and all generalizations are tedious."[24] Finally, since Father Time suggests the wearying effect of centuries of civilization and its discontents, his death can be seen as symbolic of the death of mechanical, historical clock-time in the new novel. For the experiments which are about to begin in the work of Conrad, Ford, Proust, Woolf, Joyce, and Lawrence, are attempts to break through the conceptual bonds of measured time to a more immediate subjective contact with the present physical world. If the naturists who follow Hardy create totally different styles and structures, they all seek in some manner to respond to Hardy's anguished plea for an end to the tyranny of historical time.

Hardy was well acquainted with Pascal's *Pensées*; and in Jude, it is as though he had taken Pascal's "espirit de géométrie" – the quantitative, logical, measuring faculty of man – and exaggerated it beyond Pascal's meaning, to make it the sole source of human misery. The "espirit de finesse," which for Hardy is the healthful spontaneity of nature, has died with Father Time. The plot structure of *Jude* enforces this deadening geometrical effect; for the novel is constructed around rigorous and elaborate linear parallels and oppositions that seem finally to crush the characters. Albert Guerard marvels "that the book manages to survive its almost geometrical construction";[25] but the tight, trap-like plotting is fundamental to the irony of the novel. Hardy's impassioned attack on abstract thought, then, finds its most powerful expression in the structure of his last novel. Hardy's architectural training underlies the *saeve indignatio* of *Jude the Obscure*. And Father Time, the flattest and most geometrical character in all Hardy's fiction, marks a moment when Hardy's desire to "edify" leads him to break through the bounds of credibility into a world of macabre fantasy. Father Time is all symbol – inhuman, denatured.

In spite of the despairing portrait of Father Time, Hardy repeatedly calls himself a meliorist: "If way to a Better there be, it exacts a full look at the Worst: that is to say, by the exploration of reality and its frank recognition stage by stage along the survey, with an eye to the best consummation possible: briefly, evolutionary meliorism. But it is called pessimism nevertheless. . . ."[26]

The progress of Hardy's fiction substantiates his claim: his grow-ing attention to social injustices – as distinct from his earlier tend-ency to confound natural and positive law – presumes the possibility of a way to a better world. Paradoxically, a kind of hope is projected from the fierce portrait of Father Time. The resignation of *A Pair of Blue Eyes* has given way, in *Jude*, to a more engaged indignation, an impatient search for some relief from the tragedy of most men's lives. Hardy clearly wanted a radical reorganization of society, though it is doubtful that he had any clear concept of what that society might be. We are not surprised to learn from an occasional note-book entry that Hardy's new society will allow for a greater toler-ance for the natural variety of human instinct and behavior: "I consider a social system based on individual spontaneity to promise better for happiness than a curbed and uniform one under which all temperaments are bound to shape themselves to a single pattern of living. To this end I would have society divided into *groups of tem-peraments*, with a different code of observances for each group" (*Life*, 63). Hardy's better world will emerge from the spontaneity of living things themselves: above all, from the physical nature of man, which is the foundation and guide to Hardy's spirituality. Hardy is not merely echoing the thoughts of Rousseau. His plea is not for a primitive state of nature, but for the redress of an imbalance between the individual and society. His concept of nature looks, not to the dead past, but to the evolving future. Thus Hardy's popular reputa-tion as an uncompromising pessimist is – as popular reputations often are – false.

Hardy's primary gift to the naturist novelists is the symbolism of landscape and of biological *élan* which supports and expresses in fictional form his evolutionary meliorism. For Hardy repeatedly in-sists that man has only begun to understand the mystery of nature which holds a firm hope for a better life. " 'Tis the gospel of the body," avers the rustic Joseph Poorgrass, in *Far from the Madding Crowd*, "without which we perish, so to speak it" (147).

The new relationship in Hardy's novels between landscape and character involves a new quality of microscopic vision and a new sensuous grasp of space. It also reflects Hardy's search for a new language of the unconscious in organic and animal life, which in turn relates to a dialectic between nature and convention, between the concrete and the abstract. This sense of oneness between man and his physical environment brings about a revival of the plot of physical pilgrimage built upon "spirit of place." Place, in turn, symbolizes the

B

hope of building a society more responsive to human nature, a society that in time will emerge, not through abstract dogma, but from "things themselves" – from the body of the earth and the creatures which live and grow upon it. All these basic themes and techniques were to be echoed and developed in the novels and travel books of the naturists. And if their emphasis was different from Hardy's, it was because Hardy had gone before them and prepared the way.

2 Butler: The New Spirit

Hardy's landscape is a place of refuge, an escape from the pressures and prohibitions of modern civilization. His heroes and heroines tend to merge with the landscape and become one with natural creation. Power of place delivers them – however momentarily – from the terrors of purpose and choice.

Hardy is ultimately questioning the traditional Christian view of human freedom. He believes that modern civilization has under-estimated the environmental forces which work upon man. His characters come to grief because they are unknowing victims of a Christian idealism which, in exalting free choice, provides a strong incentive for "willing to will" (as Augustine was in love with love). Thus Hardy's characters are victims of the illusion that will-power can and should vigorously tame and subdue instinct.

Freedom, Hardy seems to be saying, is not opposed to nature nor independent of it. Freedom is within nature; it is a fulfillment of instinct itself; its goal is the maturing of man's natural potentialities. Hardy is pleading for a relocation of the traditional boundary between free choice and determinism; he is claiming that human motivation is itself largely determined by the circumstances of a man's life. His novels are part of a broad attempt to reassess human nature. The focal point of this reassessment is that same Hebraic command-ment which Jude restored from obscurity: "Thou shalt not."

From the time of his earliest stories, Hardy had evoked a world of temporary refuge from the gravities of morality. Thus the author of the first general critique of Hardy's fiction paid a special tribute to an "instinct of nature worship" and a "quality of freshness," both of which reminded him of Emily Brontë. But the critic noticed an impor-tant difference between Hardy and the earlier novelists: where the Brontës and George Eliot are "ethical," in Hardy's novels "morals, observe, do not come in."[1]

This first general treatment of Hardy's novels was the first pub-lished work of a twenty-four-year-old medical student named Henry

Havelock Ellis, who was at the beginning of a career which would provide a bridge between Hardy and Lawrence, a bridge between the fiction of the nineteenth and twentieth centuries. Havelock Ellis gave a new, more specifically scientific emphasis to Hardy's "earth-consciousness"; what had been implicit in Hardy's reverently "microscopic" images became factuāl and explicit in Ellis's discursive prose. Ellis reinforced and lent scientific authority to Hardy's affirmation of the rights of instinct. Ellis's words of praise for Hardy – "morals, observe, do not come in" – might be taken as a key to his own writing, for he was among the first scientist-writers to create an atmosphere of objectivity in the discussion of sexual life.

Ellis prepared his article on Hardy with the thoroughness he was later to show in his pioneering studies of sexual behavior: he studied Barnes's dialect poems, and made a walking tour of Dorset to get "a grip of Hardy's environment." His reward was a warm letter from the novelist, praising his "remarkable paper."[2] Hardy was not among the five literary figures around whom Ellis built his first book, *The New Spirit* (1890); but the article on Hardy, though brief and restrained, was a prototype of *The New Spirit* in both theme and manner. Both works were framed as appreciative essays on "modern" authors; more importantly, both were concerned with the struggle between human instinct and human society.

In *The New Spirit*, Ellis announced with disarming self-confidence the advent of a new "renascence of the human spirit" based, like the earlier Renaissance, on a "robust faith in nature."[3] The tone of the book is one of boundless energy, fervent optimism, and considerable bravado. It is clearly written by a young man, following in the tradition of Carlyle's *Of Heroes and Hero Worship* and Emerson's *Representative Men*; just as clearly, it is written by an amateur in the field of intellectual history. Yet it is one of those books – like Burke's *On the Sublime* or Hulme's *Speculations* – which, though not of the first rank, curiously catch the mood of an age and summarize the aspirations of a new generation.

The book opens with quotations from Heraclitus and Huxley, a pair of naturists who might in fact provide a fascinating comparative study. Such a study Ellis does not provide, but his purpose is clear enough: Heraclitus' world of flux and change becomes in Huxley a biological model for change in human society itself. The passage from Huxley states the theme of Ellis's book: "There is no alleviation for the sufferings of mankind except . . . the resolute facing of the world as it is" (7). These, we recall, are the words for which Hardy provides a poetic paraphrase: "If way to a Better there be, it exacts a full look at the Worst."

Ellis's subject, then, is the Good Society. Seeking for an authority to guide man in his reconstruction of the community, Ellis turns to the earth itself and to the organic life which springs from it. The aim must be, "by searching and proving all things, to grip the earth with firmer foot-hold" (xvii). The first principle of social reform must be "that we build the lofty structure of human society on the sure and simple foundations of man's organism" (9). Human society is no longer the geometrical microcosm of Plato's *Timaeus* nor the moral arena of Dante's *De Monarchia*, nor the harmonious machine of Newton's *Principia*: society is for Ellis a biological organism. For the structure of a just society must reflect the nature of man, and Ellis and the naturists agreed wholeheartedly with Emile Zola, who had written in 1888: "The metaphysical man is dead; our whole territory is transformed by the advent of the physiological man."[4]

But if metaphysical man was dead, metaphysics was not. Ellis contends that this society-organism has continually been prodded, maimed, and tortured by authoritarian metaphysics. Like Hardy, Ellis distrusts man's faculty of reason: "The facts of life cannot be discovered by ratiocination; it is by what he *is* that man finds truth" (9). Thus, if Ellis quotes Heraclitus and Huxley, it is to the artists rather than to the philosophers that he turns for a picture of what man *is*.

Yet beneath the organic metaphor, the question remains: if we must build society on "the sure and simple foundations of man's organism," what kind of society will it be? An organic society, Ellis answers, is a socialist society. We must "socialize . . . our physical life in order that we may attain greater freedom for . . . our spiritual life" (18). *The New Spirit* exemplifies the convergence in England of two streams of nineteenth-century thought: socialism and evolutionary meliorism. The new spirit is the spirit of Shaw and Wells, and prepares the way for the utopian motif in naturist literature. Ellis was in fact one of the founders of the "Fellowship of the New Life," whose lofty purpose was "to promote the general social renovation of the world on the broadest and highest lines" (*My Life*, 203). From this society several members broke away in 1884, according to Ellis, to pursue "a more practical and political programme." The new group called themselves the Fabian Society.

The new spirit emerged from the new science, and Ellis was from the beginning a child of Darwin. He was immensely proud of the fact that he was born in 1859, the year of *Origin of Species*; his favorite childhood reading was a series of illustrated volumes entitled *Nature Displayed*; he was addicted, like Hardy and Lawrence, to interminable "walks over the hills, several times a week," which "brought fresh delicious insights into Nature" (*My Life*, 153). Finally, Ellis's seven years of medical training brought a scientific discipline which would be utilized in his later studies of sexual behavior.

Ellis's beginnings, then, were in the area of biological science, and his work is part of a huge body of popular scientific literature during these years. Huxley's influence had been enormous; but Huxley was hardly unique in his time. It is helpful to recognize the magnitude of the tide of evolutionary literature in England during the eighties. Grant Allen's *Nature Studies* (1882) is typical: it is a collection of articles on a variety of sub-human topics. Allen himself writes on "Honey Ants," "Hyacinth Bulbs," "The Origin of Buttercups," "What is a Grape?" and, charmingly, "The Beetle's view of Life." The last title has a particularly Hardyesque ring; the same humanizing note appears in James Foster's article "Birds with Teeth." Another chapter is contributed by Hardy's friend Edward Clodd who, like Allen, was one of several biographers of Darwin. Clodd's offering is a study of dreams among primitives, but he reflects a somewhat patronizing attitude – which was to be shared by Sir James Frazer – toward the odd "superstitions" of primitive peoples. Even so, Clodd's article, along with Frazer's monumental study – the first volume of which would appear in the same year (1890) as *The New Spirit* – signals a new interest in collecting material for comparative studies of primitive cultures. If anthropology has not yet arrived as a science, it is well on the way; and this revived interest in natural man is evident in the travel books of the naturists.

It is out of this background of literature that *The New Spirit* emerges; it is out of biology that a new set of sciences is born. Thus Ellis celebrates, not the pure sciences, but "the great and growing sciences of today . . . the sciences of man – anthropology, sociology . . . political economy" (*New Spirit*, 6). In the post-Freudian age it is not difficult to see why Ellis's organicism and his socialism found a focus in his continuing appeal for sexual tolerance. This very relationship is impliciit in the last novels of Hardy, and Ellis's attention to sexual repression as a primary – and unnecessary – cause of human suffering may well have begun with his early intensive reading of Hardy. His first published remarks about sexual repression occur in the Hardy article, which opens with the approving remark that

Hardy's novels "are all love stories" (356). His attention, like that of Lawrence thirty years later, is concentrated especially upon "Mr. Hardy's women," who "are creatures always fascinating, made up of more or less untamed instincts for both love and admiration, who can never help some degree of response when the satisfaction of those instincts lies open to them" (358). If Lawrence views Hardy's women with a mixture of admiration and despair, Ellis sees them as expressions of a truth never before embodied in fiction. Ellis is excited by the "quality of freshness" (350) in Hardy's women, as if Hardy were looking into the instinctual life of woman for the first time in literature.

Man's animality is his salvation: Ellis's thesis became a guiding doctrine of the naturists. Ellis's tendency to see in sexual tolerance a symbol of social happiness was shared by his close friend Edward Carpenter. Carpenter's *Love's Coming of Age* (1896) is an illuminating naturist document not only because it expands and develops themes suggested by Ellis's book, but also because Carpenter is a poet and is struggling toward a metaphorical language to convey the new spirit. His first book, *Towards Democracy*, was a lengthy volume of free verse, a shameless imitation of *Leaves of Grass*. Ellis perceptively called it "Whitman and water" (*My Life*, 204). But *Love's Coming of Age* was Whitman and science: between the earlier volume and *Love's Coming of Age* Carpenter had read widely in scientific literature, and had for several years given university extension lectures in provincial towns on biological subjects. Carpenter's continued studies are reflected in his frequent extensive revisions and additions to *Love's Coming of Age* through the edition of 1923. The fact that this edition was the twelfth is an indication that the book continued to arouse interest.

Whitman, whom Carpenter had visited in America, was also one of Ellis's "new spirits"; but where Whitman scorned the learn'd astronomer, Carpenter and Ellis were devotees, if not of the telescope, of the microscope. What Ellis and Carpenter saw in Whitman was above all his sexuality, his expression of life and growth in terms of a language of eroticism. For both, Whitman was a symbol of sexual freedom; both were highly conscious of a strain of homosexuality in Whitman. Carpenter's essay on homosexuality, "The Intermediate Sex," included in *Love's Coming of Age*, was one of the first explicit treatments of the subject, along with those of Ellis and John Addington Symonds.

It is no accident that several naturist writers were homosexual. They were not outspoken about it; to admit this preference in their time was to risk disgrace. When Carpenter asked Whitman why he was not more open about his homosexuality, Whitman refused to discuss the subject. The fall of Oscar Wilde (1895) symbolized the state of public opinion. Carpenter, Butler, Symonds, and Douglas showed more candor than was usual. T. E. Lawrence was tormented by the problem all his life. D. H. Lawrence's struggle with this "powerful but suppressed friendliness" is recorded in each of his first five novels, and memorably in "The Prussian Officer," a short story about homosexual repression. E. M. Forster was a quiet and private man; his homosexual novel *Maurice* was published only after his death. Yet the dedication of *The Longest Journey* ("Fratribus," "to the brothers") gave a hint of the theme which lay beneath the conventional surface of the novel. In later life, Forster was a member of the Wolfenden Commission, whose recommendations ultimately brought about a reform of England's harsh laws against variant sexual acts among consenting adults.

Despite their public recognition, homosexual naturists knew privately that they were social outcasts, and this realization permeates their writing. It can be seen in their passionate attack on Hebraic-Christian morality; in their admiration for pagan cultures; in their preference for biological principle over positive law; in their attempts to shock "respectable" readers; and in their use of rebels, misfits, and outsiders as heroes. These writers had reason to applaud Darwin's demonstration of the wisdom of nature in providing variants and differences – physical, sexual, and psychological – among individuals of the species. They insisted, long before Freud's work was known, that bi-sexuality was the biological foundation of human and all mammalian life, and that for this reason homosexuality could never be moralised out of existence. Most of them knew first-hand the suffering that resulted from the conventional scorn for homosexuals. These recognitions are everywhere evident in their writing, but almost always in an oblique way which avoids mention of "the love that dare not speak its name."

But there was a related theme about which they could and did write, for it had recently become acceptable in literature, and that was the servitude of women in modern life. Others of course had addressed the problem, but the homosexual approached the subject with a personal and immediate understanding. After all, he was, in popular jargon, "part woman"; he had not denied the feminine in himself. Forster typically builds his stories around a mature woman character who acts as catalyst: Mrs. Wilcox, Mrs. Moore, even Mrs.

Failing. These are women who have examined life and allowed life to examine them. Forster's novels, like Virginia Woolf's, are about women because both novelists saw how dehumanized men had become in a patriarchal civilization that "practises brutality and recommends ideals" (the phrase is Forster's). Men in these novels are the builders and makers; women tend only to live and to observe the dull, mental, specialized, masculine world of "telegrams and anger." Woolf, who often cited Coleridge's assertion that "all great minds are androgynous," places at the center of her stories a more consciously feminist woman who understands that it is not biology but civilization which has dehumanized modern men, and which has imposed upon them the myth that all males must pursue a "masculine" role. The naturist, whatever his sexual preference, applauded Hardy's call for a society more open to spontaneity, to honesty, and to variety of sexual temperament.

If *Love's Coming of Age* is a plea for sexual tolerance, the plea is soberly based on biology. Carpenter's treatment of human sexuality characteristically begins with a detailed discussion of parthenogenesis in the protozoa, "those earliest cells, the progenitors of the whole animal and vegetable kingdom,"[5] and continues with admirable evolutionary precision through infusorian reproduction in lower insects (37) to the higher forms of "conjugation" (46). The book is governed by metaphors of nutrition: sex is "hunger;" sexual expression is "nourishment;" sexual fulfillment is "growth" (35). In the metaphor is the message: sexual instinct is an organic need of the individual, and must be respected as such by the free society which Carpenter discusses in the last pages of the book.

Like Ellis, Carpenter centers his discussion upon one of the questions of the day: the emancipation of woman. Ellis had characterized modern woman as "a cross between an angel and an idiot;"[6] Carpenter writes a chapter on "Woman, the Serf." Following Ibsen, Shaw, Hardy, and George Moore, Carpenter gives a new metaphorical urgency to the problem of "present marriage customs": like Hardy's Farmer Gabriel, Carpenter's man is the oak, woman is the clinging ivy, and their relationship is a "death-struggle" (100). This is a form of combat that continues throughout naturist literature — although the roles are often significantly reversed. The inevitable and epic love-battles in the novels of Lawrence are the culmination of a tradition which includes Shaw's *Man and Superman* and Wells's *The History of Mr. Polly*.

Ellis and Carpenter, Hardy and Shaw, were pioneers in the effort to recognize that women are as free, as equal, and as sexual, as men. These writers asserted what Carpenter calls the "inner law" of the living organism as opposed to the "outer law" of social custom (5). Hardy's bold search for the roots of the affective life led him to treat sexual subjects – rapes, seductions, and problems of the marriage bed. Yet Hardy was unsure of himself when faced with the task of describing sexual encounters (given his Victorian readers, who would not be?), and tended to cover his nervousness with Latinate circumlocutions. The passage recounting Tess's seduction strikes the contemporary reader as a compound of euphemisms; and in the case of Sue Bridehead, the reader seems justified in wondering how so many children were produced. Yet Hardy's modesty was highly courageous for his time; nor does this reserve detract from his purpose, which was to reassert the essential goodness and beauty of the sexual instinct and its expression. Lawrence would elaborate Hardy's theme and give it a new direction; but if Lawrence's language is bolder it is because Huxley, Allen, Ellis, Carpenter, and their colleagues in the new spirit made the sexual act a legitimate literary subject. The secret of their effect upon popular opinion was their science: the breakthrough must be credited, not to the artist, but to the biologist.

The naturists tended to be, in one way or another, biologists. Some were geologists, others ornithologists and entomologists. Some were systematic scientists, others observers, collectors, and nature-lovers. Charles Darwin's reverent and detailed descriptions of the butterflies and birds of La Plata found an echo in the prose cadences of Hudson and Tomlinson. For others – Douglas, for example – an irreverent prose, pulsing with curiosity and punctuated with capricious non-sequiturs, reflected the style of that early Darwinian, Samuel Butler.

W. H. Hudson described himself as "a naturalist in the old, original sense of the word, one who is mainly concerned with the life and conversation of animals."[7] Joseph Conrad described Hudson as "a son of nature, an almost primitive man who was born too late."[8] R. B. Cunninghame Graham, on the contrary, thought that Hudson was "living half a century, or even more ahead of his time,"[9] an estimate that may prove to be the right one. Hudson's education as a "son of nature" began, it would seem, as soon as he began to walk, and came directly from experience. His autobiography, *Far Away and Long Ago*, consists in large part of nature description: trees, birds, weeds, butterflies. The book ends with "an event of the greatest importance in my life":[10] his brother presents him with a copy of *On the Origin of Species*, and Hudson, after a spirited struggle, is converted. It was the beginning of a long and distinguished career in science as well as literature. Hudson collected bird skins for the Smithsonian Institute, wrote articles for journals, and published *The Birds of La Plata* and the voluminous *Argentine Ornithology*. Like so many of the naturists, Hudson looked back to Hardy's Clym Yeobright for inspiration: "Do you remember Yeobright in Hardy's best work, *The Return of the Native?*" Hudson wrote to Cunninghame Graham, " – how when his eyes failed he took to cutting heath for an occupation, and was very happy in his rough toil? That would suit me better than writing."[11]

Tomlinson's eye, like Hudson's, is that of a trained naturalist. His early studies in both geology and entomology are everywhere evident in *The Sea and the Jungle*, where he describes the world of the Amazon as "elysium for the entomologist."[12] Charles M. Doughty began as a student of Suffolk chalk: "I worked a good deal with the microscope," he wrote to a scientific correspondent, "and that was in a chalk country."[13] His biographer, D. G. Hogarth, reports that Doughty "was devoted to natural science generally. He had made a large collection of Suffolk fossils and was rather combative in favour of the new studies" (4). He read geology at Cambridge, and studied glaciers and glaciation in Norway. He "was always reading geology and philosophy" (6) – an interdisciplinary combination in which almost all the naturists indulged.

H. G. Wells underwent an intensive period of reading in physiology and geology with Byatt, and later studied biology under the great Huxley himself. His first published works were articles for London scientific journals, and his first published book was a biology text. In 1942, near the end of a distinguished literary career, Wells returned to the University of London, where he was awarded the D.Sc. His dissertation, published in 1944, possessed the forbidding title "A Thesis on the Quality of Illusion in the Continuity of the Individual Life in the Higher Metazoa, with Particular Reference to the Species Homo Sapiens."[14]

Where Wells was throughout his life an enthusiastic student of the physical sciences, D. H. Lawrence would hotly disapprove the mechanistic rationalism of the scientific method, from Bacon to Freud. Yet as a young teacher at Croydon School, Lawrence's subject was "Nature-Study"; and his novels and travel books make clear that he remained all his life an avid student of nature.

Norman Douglas began a study of minerals and fossils at Karlsruhe; he would later write on the pumice stone of the Lipari Islands.

He was both geologist and ornithologist: his first printed essay was called "Variations of Plumage in the Corvidiae." There followed a series of zoological papers, the most ambitious being a study of snakes and reptiles in the Grand Duchy of Baden. Douglas's attention, in this paper, to the sexual function of secondary physical characteristics led to his later essay, *On the Darwinian Hypothesis of Sexual Selection*,[15] an examination of the coloring of lizards. Douglas's choice of subject-matter for scientific study was a kind of symbol of the man himself: he was one of the few writers in history to have made valid scientific investigation an erotic experience. His *Paneros*, a painstaking but witty study of aphrodisiacs, is an example of the new spirit pursued with a vengeance. Yet *Paneros* should be read along with *South Wind*, and in this respect it is typical: the scientific writings of the naturists make superb commentaries on, and excellent introductions to, their travel books and novels.

The scientific interests of these writer-naturalists will radically affect both the conscious purpose and the prose technique of their travelogues, novels, and utopian fantasies. They will inherit from Hardy an imagery of organism. But their new technical sophistication in matters of Darwinian science, as well as their new utopian preoccupations, suggest their indebtedness to another presiding spirit of naturism, Samuel Butler.

For Butler's influence, if controversial, was enormous. Grant Allen, for example, felt obliged to state, in the preface of his biography of Darwin: "From Mr. Samuel Butler, the author of 'Evolution Old and New,' I have derived many pregnant suggestions."[16] This is a noteworthy acknowledgement that beneath Allen's disagreement with Butler lay a considerable debt.

But the debt of the naturists to Butler was greater; for Butler used, with varying degrees of success, all the literary forms which will be dear to the naturists – the scientific essay, the philosophic essay, the notebook, the travel book, the utopian fantasy, the novel. If Hardy's microscopic vision revealed an implicit hope for the future, Butler's microscope attained the prophetic power of a Tiresias. Butler's fictional scientists anticipate a time when "it would be possible, by examining a single hair with a powerful microscope, to know whether its owner could be insulted with impunity."[17]

If some naturists make disparaging remarks about Butler, their quarrel is all the more in the filial spirit of Butler's own sharp quarrel with father Darwin. Yet the new writers tend to confirm Butler's position in the Lamarkian controversy; they seek, with

Butler, Hardy, and Shaw, a creative mind in nature. They also inherit Butler's imaginative attempt to apply the techniques of experimental science to the reorganization of society. Ellis, Carpenter, Hudson, Tomlinson, Wells, Douglas, Lawrence – all have as their central concern a free society. As they write about stone formations, or metazoa, or butterflies or birds or lizards, they are simultaneously commenting on education and the family, economics and the machine, politics and freedom, middle-class mores and mental health.

These writers are dedicated to the physical world in and for itself; but their nature description, like Butler's, betrays their continual search, through microscopes and field glasses, for Utopia, for a New Atlantis whose pattern must derive, not from the stratospheric regions of theology and metaphysics, but from beneath, from the land itself. Theirs is a topsy-turvy Utopia, where the kingly sciences give way to the grubbing, mundane science of biology. Theirs is a new upside-down Utopia, transformed from Greek to English, and spelled backwards: Erewhon.

E. M. Forster, in an essay called "A Book that Influenced Me," wrote of Samuel Butler's *Erewhon*: "It opens with some superb descriptions of mountain scenery."[18] Forster's remark serves to remind us that Butler is an expert landscape artist. The reader is likely to forget, for example, that *Erewhon* is framed at the beginning and the end by sustained passages of landscape description. At first reading, the opening five chapters of the book, which describe the mountain-pilgrimage into Erewhon, seem unnecessary: the reader is impatient to arrive. But the topographical prelude is essential: we enter Utopia through landscape:

> I am there now as I write; I fancy that I can see the downs, the huts, the plain, and the river-bed – that torrent pathway of desolation, with its distant roar of waters. Oh, wonderful, wonderful! so lonely and so solemn, with the sad gray clouds above, and no sound save a lost lamb bleating upon the mountain side, as though its little heart were breaking. (21)

Butler's narrator finds the desolation "wonderful," and dwells on the words "lonely," "solemn," and "sad" with a blissful passion of rediscovery. In 1876 – four years after the publication of *Erewhon* – Hardy suggested that "the new Vale of Tempe may be a gaunt waste in Thule; the time is near, if it has not actually arrived, when the chastened sublimity of a moor, a sea, or a mountain will be all of nature that is absolutely in keeping with the moods of the more thinking among mankind" (*Return*, 13).

The time had actually arrived. Butler, in *Erewhon* and *Alps and Sanctuaries*, had located Hardy's "chastened sublimity." The search for the "gaunt waste" continued: a decade later Charles Doughty devoted a thousand pages to detailed descriptions of the Arabian desert; Norman Douglas, T. E. Lawrence, and Cunninghame Graham, among others, shared Doughty's fascination with sun-baked sand. Hudson, meanwhile, had been attracted to the bare desolation of Patagonia.

Butler's literary landscape, like his fine pen-and-ink sketches in *Alps and Sanctuaries*, have a special quality of distance from civilization. Erewhon itself, like the bodies of its inhabitants, is beautiful: Butler's Utopia is founded on a spare, stark, physical beauty and physical health. Crime is an illness in Erewhon, and illness is a crime. The community is built upon the principle that "the body is everything" (118).

In Erewhon, the faculty of reason is attributed to the unreasoning, thought to the unthinking organism. Butler is utilizing the language of science in an attempt to explore the unconscious life of man. More specifically, he is asserting that "unreason is part of reason" (163), that the logical way is the absurd way. The Erewhonian "Professor of Unreason" (164) is Butler himself: he not only insists that the creative faculty in man is organic and unconscious, he also endows animal and vegetable life with a form of "intelligence, either spent and now unconscious, or still unspent and conscious" (208). Living perfection is always for Butler unconscious: any living creature "will become unconscious as soon as the skill that directs it has become perfected" (212). Thus the Erewhonian Professor of Botany in the College of Unreason takes as his text "the one in which our Lord tells His disciples to consider the lilies of the fields, who neither toil nor spin . . ." (212). Butler's narrator considers the lilies for a while and decides that "there had been no lack of either toiling or spinning": it took intelligence, he reasons, for the lilies to succeed so perfectly where Solomon in all his glory had so abysmally failed. Butler takes the gospel statement literally: the lilies are indeed the teachers of men.

The words "consider the lilies" might stand in fact as the device for the naturist movement. Mrs. Yeobright, four years after *Erewhon*, scrutinizes the "wild ephemerons"; Ellis and Carpenter observe the protozoa, Hudson the finches, Tomlinson the butterflies, Douglas the lizards. D. H. Lawrence comes full circle: he re-examines the lily itself in *Women in Love*, and decides that "the final aim is the flower" ("Study," 403); he praises Hardy's characters for "taking no thought for the morrow, but at evening, considering the ruddy lily" ("Study," 398); and in *Aaron's Rod* he creates a spokesman for wisdom – critics agree that the character is Lawrence himself – who is named Rawdon Lilly.

Erewhon is built upon a single basic conceit: the reversal of physical for moral and moral for physical being. In the world of post-Reformation Christianity, moral virtue tended to be defined in terms of bodily self-denial. In Erewhon, where the body is everything, bodily health tends to be defined in terms of the denial of Calvinist morality. Moral judgement, in fact, is the chief cause of illness (our "crime") in Erewhon: ". . . the greater part of the illness which exists in their country is brought about by the insane manner in which it is treated" (100); moral severity, Butler argues, leads to concealment, and concealment aggravates disease. Like alcohol, "unalloyed virtue is not a thing to be immoderately indulged in" (87). In Butler's good society, the first article of faith is allegiance to organic process. Idealistic morality, in denying the organism, becomes a kind of virulent disease. Friedrich Nietzsche, who was an avid reader of English literature, would make Butler's idea his own in the years following the publication of *Erewhon*.

Butler's fantasy reflects conventional values in the reversed manner of a mirror, just as its title, held before a mirror, spells, after a fashion, "nowhere." Lewis Carroll's *Through the Looking Glass*, published the same year as *Erewhon* (1872), presents, in a similar mood of fantasy, a similar reversed-mirror image. Both titles announce the beginning of a revolt whose method will be to shock by reversing the enshrined platitudes of Christian humanism. Both titles reflect, like a mirror, the shifting mood of the time.

That mood, which culminated in the work of the naturists, was the temper of the new spirit: the open rebellion against the Cartesian proposition, which had dominated the Western imagination for two hundred years, that "l'âme, par lequel je suis ce que je suis, est entièrement distincte du corps"[19] ("the soul, by which I am what I am, is entirely distinct from the body"). Butler reversed the status of "mind" and "body," not to perpetuate the dualism, but to jar his reader into a recognition of the unity underlying the verbal dichotomy. This Butler meant quite literally: it was the basis of his "Lamarkianism."

The dualities which abound ' in *Erewhon* — body–mind, reason–unreason, illness–crime – have a quite different function from the oppositions involved in the technique of neo-classical satire. For Pope, the relationship between image and idea was clearly in the spirit of Descartes; Pope's purpose was to convey the "Something whose truth convinced at sight we find / That gives us back the image of our mind." For Pope or Molière, that "something" was invariably the mirror-image of an incongruous extreme which reflected, through excess, a central insight into truth. The pratfall in Molière illustrated negatively the truth of Newton's laws of gravitation. Swift's Laputans, talking with things, mirrored the inanity of materialistic philosophies. But where the Laputans are objects of Swift's ridicule, Butler's Erewhonians are edifying examples, rather than satiric targets.

Swift's Laputans may clumsily talk with material objects, but material objects talk in *Erewhon*: "The potato says these things by doing them, which is the best of languages. What is consciousness if this is not consciousness?" (175). Butler's method here is far from satiric: his Erewhonians provide a mirror-perspective which, though opposite to ours, contains a truth we have missed. Swift's humor derives from incongruity, and incongruity to Swift is falsehood. Butler's incongruity is truth: he is saying, with Shaw's Keegan, in *John Bull's Other Island*, "My way of joking is to tell the truth. It's the funniest joke in the world."

Butler's "looking glass" is more than a mind reflector, more than an image projecting an idea. It is an attempt to break down the Cartesian wall between "la substance étendue" ("extended substance") and "la substance qui pense" ("thinking substance"). Butler's method, to be sure, is itself Cartesian: he has reversed the neo-classical opposition between body and mind in order to challenge it.

Butler's affinity, then, is not with the great neo-classical satirists. It is rather with those pre-Reformation humanists who were seeking a new language of nature: Erasmus, More, Skelton. More's Utopians, like Butler's Erewhonians, are embodiments of a healthy allegiance to nature. In More's fantasy, nature is in fact the primary source of morality: "They define virtue as living according to nature," says Hythloday about the Utopians.[20] More's society is built in harmony with the basic requirements of physical life. The primary good for More's Utopians, upon which all spiritual life was to be based, is pleasure.

Butler and the writers of the new spirit follow in the naturist tradition of More and Erasmus. When Ellis speaks of socializing the physical life to attain freedom for the spiritual life, he is paraphrasing More's Utopian socialistic laws of distribution: "For such laws determine the distribution of goods, and goods are a prerequisite of pleasure" (*Utopia*, 49). Similarly Butler, in making disease a crime, is turning back to More's emphasis on physical health, upon which the whole Utopian hierarchy of pleasure rests: "If it [health] is lacking, there is no chance for any other pleasure" (*Utopia*, 51).

In these respects, and many others, there is a striking analogy between the aims of the age of More and the age of Butler and Hardy. It is as though the new spirit were an attempt to resume work which had been interrupted by the Reformation, by the new rationalism, and by industrialism. The interruption had lasted, in spite of the Romantic movement, for over three hundred years, and the Calvinist–Cartesian way of conceiving reality had become, as Whitehead has shown, a universal presupposition. Butler's appropriation of More's devices and his themes is typical of the continual presence of early Renaissance names and motifs in the writing of the naturists. The opening sentence of *The New Spirit* sets the mood: "There is a remarkable period in the history of Europe which we call the Renaissance . . ." (4). Thus Charles Doughty spends a year in Holland out of reverence for the memory of Erasmus and Scaliger. Thus E. M. Forster writes an appreciative essay on Skelton, and confesses that "my law-givers are Erasmus and Montaigne, not Moses and St Paul" (*Two Cheers*, 67). Thus Tomlinson looks back to Drake, Hawkins, and Raleigh; on the Madeira he discovers a modern equivalent of Rabelais' Thélèmes, where there are no walls: "There were no fences and no private bounds . . . it was a warm, a living body" (*Sea and Jungle*, 129). Havelock Ellis indeed appropriates Thélèmes as his utopian model: "I look for the coming of Thélema and I accept its ethical rule, 'Fays ce que vouldras' " (*My Life*, 111). Hudson and Lawrence write novels whose themes might have been taken from Montaigne's oft-repeated conviction that "la plupart de nos vocations sont farcesques" ("most of our vocations are farcical"); while the writings of Butler and Douglas constitute a continual paean in praise of "folly."

Lawrence finds in the Etruscans the same pre-Socratic freshness and freedom which is so often associated with the early Renaissance. That perspective, to be sure, does an injustice to the complexity of the Renaissance spirit. Since the time of Burckhardt, scholars have looked more closely at the sceptical side of the Renaissance. Today we can recall, for example, that Montaigne quotes the Book of Ecclesiastes more often than any other. But the new spirit writers are hardly forgetful of the evanescence of all things human. Hardy in his diaries and novels seems often to be listening to the words of Ecclesiastes the Preacher: "Vanity of vanities, all is vanity." And Havelock Ellis ends his introductory call for a new Renaissance with some prudent, and typically Renaissance, advice: "Set your shoulder joyously to the world's wheel: you may spare yourself some unhappiness if, beforehand, you slip the book of Ecclesiastes beneath your arm" (*New Spirit*, 33).

Renaissance humanists from Rabelais to More were seeking new literary forms to express this renewed reverence for life. They were deeply convinced of the binding continuity between the wisdom of physical nature, on the one hand, and problems of human behavior and social organization, on the other. Pantagruel, Stultitia, and Hythloday struggled to speak a new language, a language which finally came to fruition in such a work as Shakespeare's *The Tempest*.

This Renaissance search for the Lost Atlantis where man might again let nature be his guide forms an illuminating parallel to the aspirations of the naturists. In both epochs the central problem was language. Erasmus and More sought, by means of a revival of the Greek language, to break through the tyranny of Church Latin, and the view of the world it embodied. They sought to create a new idiom to express the needs of the natural man. So it was with the naturists: they felt that an essential dimension of human experience had been neglected and discounted – the part of man's nature which connects him with the physical world. Their task was to forge an idiom, a symbolism, and a myth to embody this lost vision.

The language they created was a language of place, an identification of human emotions and attitudes with geographical location, topography and climate, flora and fauna, native culture and mores. This naturist abandonment to place was a symptom of that same cast of mind which led Butler to assert the primacy of body over mind, of things over ideas, of health over virtue. This new generation of writers were physiographers, after the spirit and technique of Thomas Hardy; they were preoccupied with the language of organic change, in the manner of the new spirit; they were utopians of the body, in the tradition of Samuel Butler. All shared with Hardy and Butler a distrust of ratiocination and a reverence for the sexual instinct. Most wrote novels whose structure and symbolism were totally determined by "spirit of place." All were restless voyagers in the adventurous spirit of Tomlinson's Jack Hawkins. They recorded their discoveries in a series of travel books which provides an essential key to the spirit of Edwardian fiction. For these travel books provide a record, not only of the lands they describe, but also of a quality of vision: they provide the pattern for a new kind of novel.

These travelogues were written to entertain, and they are patently escapist. But the escape from industrial middle-class England was for these writers also a search for roots in physical reality. Their pilgrimage was both an idle recreation and a serious course of research. The title of Samuel Butler's own travel book, *Alps and Sanctuaries*, symbolizes this twofold nature of the new travel literature: if the sanctuary is a place of refuge, the Alpine promontories betoken both a challenge and a bold aspiration.

3 Spirit of Place: The Travel Book

Hardy's Via Iceniana, the great Western road which crossed Egdon Heath, was the product of a great imperialist power. So too was the road travelled by Englishmen, late in the reign of Victoria, to every part of her empire. But if Victorian travel literature owed its existence to a highly industrialized and civilized power, it provided an escape from that same power and that same civilization. It is not my purpose to survey that voluminous literature, but rather to indicate that travel books of the period 1895–1920 continue a well-established tradition that would include such Victorian travellers as Robert Louis Stevenson, John Addington Symonds, Lafcadio Hearn, and Sir Leslie Stephens.

Edwardian travel literature tends to focus on three geographical areas: Italy, South America, and the desert belt stretching from Arabia across North Africa. Edwardian writers about Italy looked to Samuel Butler's *Alps and Sanctuaries* as a prototype; South American travellers found an authoritative precedent in Charles Darwin's *Voyage of the Beagle*; the desert school followed in the path of Charles M. Doughty's formidable *Travels in Arabia Deserta*. Of the first group, Norman Douglas and D. H. Lawrence are perhaps the outstanding examples; of the second, W. H. Hudson and H. M. Tomlinson; in the third – and by far the largest – group might be included Wilfrid Blunt, E. G. Browne, David Hogarth, R. B. Cunninghame Graham, T. E. Lawrence, and Norman Douglas. Yet the literature of the Arab world produced no important piece of English fiction – unless, that is, we wish to read T. E. Lawrence's *The Seven Pillars of Wisdom* as fiction, as some historians are inclined to do. It was the French novelist – Gide, in *The Immoralist*, or Camus, in *The Stranger* and *The Plague* – who exploited this vein. Thus our discussion will center upon the literature of Italy, which will include such travel books as *Old Calabria* or *Sea and Sardinia*, and upon such South American travelogues as *Idle Days in Patagonia*, or *The Sea and the Jungle*.

A further distinction might be made between the traveller as expatriate and as English citizen. Hudson and Tomlinson travel round-trip; their voyages begin and end in London, and this fact has an effect upon both the tone and structure of their books. But Douglas and Lawrence are wandering exiles: they convey the impression of having no home in England, no place to return, and thus the structure of their travel books — and novels — tends to have a serial quality whereby the movement of the traveller seems to extend beyond the limits of the story itself.

My purpose is to emphasize those conventions of travel literature which have to do importantly with the new "travel novel." This emphasis in no way carries the implication that Edwardian travel literature is not a delight and an end in itself: indeed, it might be argued that the travelogues of this period rank among the finest in all English literature. But if the Edwardian travel writer tends to succeed where the travel novelist fails, it is because the aims of the novelist are more ambitious and more difficult; and the Edwardian travel novel too has its origin in the age of Victoria; such romances as Rider Haggard's *King Solomon's Mines*, Stevenson's *Treasure Island*, and Anthony Hope's *The Prisoner of Zenda* have provided a precedent, at least in terms of locale. But the main channel of Victorian fiction has been urban and domestic, and emerges from a point of view within English culture. With Hardy the English novel moves out of the Victorian parlor on to the open road; and the naturist novelist will follow that road to the outskirts of civilization.

The travel tale is hardly new to English literature: from Chaucer to Mandeville, from Hakluyt to Captain John Newton, from Nashe's Jack Wilton to Smollett's Roderick Random, from Sterne's sentimental voyager to George Borrow's gypsy wanderer, the travel book — both as fiction and as reportage — had waxed and waned with an impressive durability. In each case the travel story had reflected the special values and aspirations of the time. So it was with the naturist travelogue: a traditional genre was transformed to meet a new and urgent need.

The earlier picaresque travel hero tends either to perpetrate (like Jack Wilton) or to suffer endlessly (like Roderick Random) from a series of those human deceptions and rogueries which have no geographical boundaries. The picaresque tale is a battle of wits among individuals, each seeking an identity within society. The new twentieth-century travel hero escapes the treacheries, not of individuals, but of society itself, and his goal is contemplative isolation rather

than success in the world of men. When an eighteenth-century way-
farer like Robinson Crusoe has the misfortune to be cast upon a lonely
island, he overcomes the obstacles of his environment by means of
his own vitality and ingenuity. The new travel hero, on the contrary,
is the passive recipient of a wisdom which resides, not in the crafts
of civilized man, but in physical nature itself. Geographical movement provides, for Roderick Random, a mechanical framework and a
background for human action; in the new novel, the central human
action is to see, to meditate, and to learn from landscape, which is
the "principal personage" of the tale.

Hardy's prediction, in *Return of the Native*, that "the new Vale of
Tempe may be a gaunt waste in Thule" – that the new tourist would
find his mood reflected by landscapes of "sombreness" and "desolation" (5) – proved during the following decades to be unusually prophetic. Samuel Butler's landscapes were, like Egdon, remarkable for
their quality of barren grandeur, their lonely and solemn distance
from civilization. Butler's "torrent pathway of desolation" to Erewhon remains a dominating image in *Alps and Sanctuaries*, for
Butler's Italian Alps tend to surround, dominate, and almost hide
his ecclesiastical sanctuaries. His fine pen-and-ink sketches betray
his mood perhaps more than does his mercurial prose. His drawing,
for example, of the Chapel of Saint Carlo, Piora,[1] shows in the fore-
ground a small stream with a tiny foot-bridge; a woman hobbles
under a heavy load, a cane in her hand; a man is herding a few dis-
consolate cattle. In the center of the drawing is a tiny, toy-like building: it is the chapel. But the humans and their artifacts are utterly
dwarfed by a line of bare Alpine peaks against an unending cloudless
sky. Again, his sketch of Calonico church (47) shows only a portion
of roof and a low bell-tower, pinioned by bushes, trees, and mountain-
side. We can hear Butler exclaiming, with his Erewhonian narrator,
"Oh wonderful, wonderful!"

These same qualities had already produced the same wonder in
the heart of Charles Darwin when, during his early twenties, he had
found in the plains of Patagonia his own "gaunt waste in Thule."
Darwin would never forget that sight; it would hold a meaning for
him which would become a common theme for the travel writers who
would take Darwin's *Voyage of the Beagle* for a model. Darwin's
self-questioning about his reaction to the "wretched and useless"
Patagonian wastes marks the beginning of a special genre of travel
book:

. . . the plains of Patagonia frequently cross before my eyes; yet these plains are pronounced by all to be most wretched and useless . . . without habitations, without water, without trees, without mountains, they support only a few dwarf plants. Why, then – and the case is not peculiar to myself – have these arid wastes taken so firm possession of my mind? . . . I can scarce analyse these feelings, but it must be partly owing to the free scope given to the imagination. The plains of Patagonia are boundless, for they are scarcely practicable, and hence unknown . . . there appears no limit to their duration through future time. If, as the ancients supposed, the flat earth was surrounded by an impassable breadth of water, by deserts heated to an intolerable excess, who would not look at these last boundaries to man's knowledge with deep but ill-defined sensations?[2]

These "ill-defined sensations" of boundlessness and timelessness become the central subject of naturist travel literature. W. H. Hudson, for example, recapitulates Darwin's theme at the beginning of *Idle Days*;[3] and toward the end of the book, Hudson includes the passage from Darwin quoted above, a passage "which, for me, has a very special interest and significance." For Hudson's trip began with his reading of Darwin's *Voyage of the Beagle*. Patagonia took possession of Hudson's mind as it had Darwin's, and induced a state of "suspense and watchfulness," where "thought had become impossible" (199). Hudson's language reminds us of Hardy's Egdon Heath, "full of watchful intentness." And when H. M. Tomlinson later finds in the jungle a quality of "vacancy of large composure, with a lofty watchfulness which has no need to show its mind" (*Sea and Jungle*, 106), we recognize a similarity of idiom which, if it is not the result of light plagiarism, is surely representative of a striking community of mind.

A like suspension of mind overtook Norman Douglas as he finished his travels through Old Calabria "in the breathless hush of noon" when "the silence can be felt."[4] "Such torrid splendour," wrote Douglas, "drenching a land of austerest simplicity, decomposes the mind into corresponding states of primal contentment and resilience" (461). It is characteristic that this experience gave Douglas a glimpse of the better society of the future: "There arises before our phantasy a new perspective of human affairs; a suggestion of well-being wherein the futile complexities and disharmonies of our age shall have no place" (461).

Hardy, Darwin, Hudson, Tomlinson, Douglas – all saw the same quality of landscape: a knowledge beyond that of man, greater, wiser, more mysterious. When they looked at brute matter, they saw what Darwin saw: the unknown. Thus for Tomlinson the landscape of Brazil contained "the prescience of destiny, as though an eyeless mask sat at the table with us, but though it stays, makes no sign" (*Sea and Jungle*, 135). Thus for Hudson the landscape infused a receptivity of mind, a state of waiting for a message, "a revelation of an unfamiliar and unsuspected nature hidden under the nature we are conscious of" (*Idle Days*, 200). Thus D. H. Lawrence wrote of a Tuscan hill: "And immediately one feels: that hill has a soul, it has a meaning."[5]

This same feeling for the attractiveness of desolation was in large part responsible for a new and special branch of travel literature: the story of the desert. Doughty's *Arabia Deserta*, though it was not the first, was the best book on the subject, and it, along with Doughty's other books, was vastly admired at the turn of the century. Hudson praised *Arabia Deserta* to Garnett, whose abridgement of Doughty's work (*Wanderings in Arabia*, 1908) ran into several editions. Hudson also admired Doughty's *Dawn in Britain*, as did D. H. Lawrence. But Lawrence's favorite Doughty work was *Adam Cast Forth*, for in it he found an image which would become the central theme of his fiction. "He sent me," wrote Jessie Chambers, "Charles Doughty's *Adam Cast Forth*, and I was especially to note where Eve, after long separation, finds Adam, and he tells her to bind herself to him with the vine strands, lest they be separated again by the Wind of God."[6]

Certainly Doughty was one of those indomitable eccentrics who have always flourished in English culture. He attempted to outdo Milton, but no reader would wish Doughty's interminable epic to be any longer. Yet when Doughty shifts his attention and his imagination from poetry to geology, he becomes indeed poetic and creative. His *Arabia Deserta* is a highly original and powerful evocation of the spaces and contours of the desert land. Doughty sees, in these "boundless and bare, lone and level sands," what others had ignored or found monotonous: the desert becomes alive in its desolation. Doughty's book inspired a generation of desert enthusiasts, of whom the most prominent was Doughty's young friend Lawrence of Arabia, who carried *Arabia Deserta* with him on his desert journeys.

Norman Douglas wrote a chapter on Doughty's *Deserta* in *Experiments*; and Tomlinson's choice of the two greatest writers of his

time is startling and illuminating: Thomas Hardy and Charles M.
Doughty.[7] Tomlinson's pairing may seem odd, but Doughty's book
was written with that same earth-reverence to be found in Hardy.
Doughty's own description of his book is characteristic, for the description begins and ends, like *Return of the Native* and *Erewhon*,
with earth and rocks, framing and diminishing humanity. Doughty
describes *Arabia Deserta* as "the Story of the Earth, Her manifold
living creatures, the human generations and Her living rocks."[8]
Doughty's work is a story in two senses: it is both a pilgrimage-
adventure and a topological-geological study. The mass of detail
assembled by Doughty is framed and ordered by the author's own
physical movement, his adventure. Thus Tomlinson, writing in 1931,
admired the book because for him it described a universal human experience: "A poet's collected work, a novelists's series of tales, as
well as the *Arabia Deserta*, may be classed as travel literature,
whether or not we like the country" (*Douglas*, 34). For the naturist,
all good literature is travel literature: like D. H. Lawrence, Tomlinson saw even Whitman's book of poems as a kind of travelogue: "Is
not *Leaves of Grass* a survey of a new continent?" (34). But Tomlinson's highest tribute was reserved for Norman Douglas as a travel
writer: "He knows his earth, though it gives him a little less joy
when we crowd the scene" (61). "To know his earth" is the highest
goal of the naturist travel writer: "You could smell this good earth,"
Tomlinson would exclaim (*Sea and Jungle*, 119); and Hudson would
exult: "And that was the life I desired – the life the heart can con-
ceive – the earth life" (*Far Away*, 347).

 Thus Norman Douglas chose, for his longest and best travel book,
a region he calls "the Sahara of Italy" (*Old Calabria*, 8), a land of
"austerest simplicity," beset with poverty and malaria. "This corner
of Magna Graecia," he wrote, "is a severely parsimonious manifestation of nature. Rocks and waters!" (462). The reason for Douglas's
loving and detailed description of these rocks and waters might
well be taken as the credo of all the naturists: "But these rocks and
waters are actualities; the stuff whereof man is made. A landscape
so luminous, so resolutely scornful of accessories, hints at brave and
simple forms of expression; it brings us to the ground, where we
belong" (462). Douglas's contention that man is made of rocks and
waters not only reflects his early zoological studies, it also betrays
his deep indebtedness to Samuel Butler, for whom "the body is
everything." The writings of Douglas can in fact be seen as a twentieth-century extension of the spirit of Samuel Butler. The two men

are strikingly akin temperamentally: both are passionate eccentrics, riders of hobby horses, collectors of trivia, antiquarians, expert biologists, inveterate travellers, and genteel rebels against prevailing mores. Butler's biological interests are echoed in Douglas's early writings; indeed Keith, in *South Wind*, urges young Denis to read only Butler: "I took him up, I remember," Keith says, "during my biological period" (125). Douglas follows Butler's Lamarkian bias in his early scientific writings, and both writers display in their travel books a sharp sense of botanical gamesmanship that verges on pedantry. Butler discovers, for example, "the rare English fern Woodsia hyperborea," and "one specimen of Asplenium alternifolium" (*Alps*, 18); and Douglas, not to be outdone, notes in *Old Calabria* no less than thirteen types of fig: "fico arnese, fico santillo, fico . . ." – and he continues ruthlessly to list all thirteen (68)).

It might be said that Butler's *Alps and Sanctuaries* is based upon that same Rabelaisian motto honored by Havelock Ellis: "Fays ce que vouldras," although Butler seems to prefer a Victorian version of the sentiment, quoting Disraeli: "There is nothing like will; everybody can do exactly what they like in this world, provided they really like it" (*Alps*, 7). Butler's book is a model of caprice: it begins with a discussion of Handel and Shakespeare (7), and continues as a rambling, disconnected series of observations on every conceivable subject. The pages of *Alps* are filled with sketches and passages of music, usually of Handel; the sight of a young Italian peasant sketching leads Butler to a lengthy consideration of "primitive" art, illustrated with three sketches by untutored Italians (114–19).

Yet Butler's book is structured around a series of revelations not unlike that of Darwin in Patagonia, or that of the Erewhonian narrator at the sight of the "desolate torrent." Thus the sound of the "roar of the Ticino" river sets "a passage from the *Messiah* sounding in my ears" – and Butler unhesitatingly prints the bars from Handel, along with a sketch, as if to use every art to fix this moment of "ill-defined" recognition (208). It is in fact a mark of the progress – or retrogression – of the naturist movement that, where Butler resorts to Handel, Hudson abandons counterpoint for the simplicity of bird-song. Yet Butler is hardly immune to the charms of the bird-call: he notices that "there was one bird, I think it was the New Zealand thrush, but am not sure, which used to sing thus" – and he proceeds to print several bars of melody (208). Characteristically, Butler is angry with the bird: unlike Handel, the thrush fails to develop the opening melodic theme properly, and Butler unhesitatingly sets down several bars of music he *wishes* the thrush had sung. This Butlerian impatience with the artistic gaffes of the ornithological world is nowhere to be found in Hudson.

Butler's treatment of illness as a crime and crime as an illness, in *Erewhon*, receives a new expression in Douglas's contention about metaphysics: "You cannot refute a disease" (*Old Calabria*, 382). Conversely, Douglas's abiding interest in food and its preparation reflects the Butlerian emphasis upon pleasures of the body. "Virtues and vices which cannot be expressed in physiological terms," writes Douglas, "are not worth talking about" (176). But where Butler's hedonism is reserved and Victorian, Douglas adds a special scatological touch: of the southern Italians, he writes: "They have a proverb which runs 'sfoga o schiatta' – relieve yourself or burst; our vaunted ideal of self-restraint, of dominating the reflexes, being thought not only fanciful but injurious to health" (180). Above all, *Old Calabria* echoes Butler's firm belief in idleness and in the wisdom of child's-play, as does Douglas's charming and fanciful collection, *London Street Games*. Like Butler, Douglas is everywhere master of the *non-sequitur*. *Old Calabria* moves from a chat with a barber to thoughts about Byzantine art to discussions of Calabrian wine. In this Douglas is typical of the naturist travel writer: words such as "careless," "idle," "drifting," "curious," abound in these travel books. The book titles are themselves suggestive of this fascination with the unpremeditated, the gratuitous, the accidental: "Idle Days," "Experiments," "Mornings in Mexico."

Douglas typically insists that "childishness" is a matter of climatic influences; he pays special note to Calabrian children's games and childish superstitions. Idleness is the supreme good: "You may spend pleasant days in this city of Cosenza, doing nothing whatever" (223). The art of doing nothing is a serious business for both Butler and Douglas. To be a "lotus eater" is a "moral duty" for Butler's Ernest Pontifex; and young Denis, at the conclusion of *South Wind*, learns the final lesson of the island from Keith: "He advised me to sit among the rocks at midnight and in the hot afternoons, conversing with the genii of earth and air" (256). But such idle contemplation, such abandonment of mind and will to the earth-spirits, is the beginning of wisdom. The concluding sentence of *Old Calabria* is both an epitaph for Butler and an introduction to *South Wind*: "From these brown stones . . . he can carve out . . . some tonic philosophy that shall foster sunny mischiefs and farewell regret" (462).

Beneath the apparent aimlessness of *Alps and Sanctuaries* and *Old Calabria* lies a serious purpose, an interior voyage of the heart. It is a journey that ends in an evolutionary beginning, when man emerged from the rocks and waters. This was the kind of voyage Douglas admired in Doughty's *Arabia Deserta*: "It seems to me," wrote Douglas about Doughty in *Experiments*, "that a reader of a good travel-book is entitled not only to an exterior voyage, to descriptions of scenery and so forth, but to an interior, a sentimental or temperamental voyage, which takes place side by side with that outer one."[9]

Douglas's insight about Doughty's book is valid: *Arabia Deserta* derives unity from a sense of destination, just as Homer's Odysseus moves through a series of episodic adventures, but always with the purposeful pull towards Ithaca and Penelope. To compare Doughty with Homer is perhaps irreverent; yet Doughty's artistic sensibility worked inevitably in a pattern of epic. After completing *Arabia Deserta*, Doughty spent many years writing a six-volume epic entitled *The Dawn in Britain*: it was Milton's discarded subject for the poem that was to become *Paradise Lost*. Doughty wrote his own version of man's fall: *Adam Cast Forth* serves to remind us that always in the back of his mind was the myth of Eden, whether it was to be found in the story of Adam, or the story of Bonduca, or the "story of Earth" in Arabia. The immense popularity of both Doughty and Hudson during the Edwardian years rests primarily upon the fact that every one of their books is built around the myth of Eden. For the story of the naturist travel book is, in fact, the story of a search for Eden. D. H. Lawrence, reviewing Tomlinson's *Gifts of Fortune*, expressed the prevailing dream of travellers from Doughty to Lawrence himself: "We travel, perhaps, with a secret and absurd hope of setting foot on the Hesperides, of running our boat up a little creek and landing in the Garden of Eden" (*Phoenix*, 343).

For modern man the search for Eden must be a movement backwards from paradise lost; thus Hudson's *Idle Days* opens with an exclamation which might be that of a fallen Adam: " 'We are lost,' I heard one say; and another answer, 'Aye, lost for ever!' " (2). It is a line that might well be found in a tale by Joseph Conrad; but where Conrad's heroes usually remain "lost for ever," Hudson's line is a prelude to the story of paradise regained. Hudson's is the story of Lazarus rising from his sepulchre, not by means of the healing words of Christ, but by means of "Nature's voices":

And we ourselves are the living sepulchres of a dead past . . . its old bones are slumbering in us dead, and yet not dead nor deaf to Nature's voices; the noisy burn, the roar of the waterfall, and the thunder of long waves on the shore, and the sound of rain and the whispering winds in the multitudinous leaves, bring it a memory of the ancient time; and the bones rejoice and dance in their sepulchre. (206)

Hudson's *recherche du temps perdu* necessarily involves the image of Eden, and we are not surprised to find, in the depths of Patagonia, Eve's serpent of temptation. But there is a difference: where the snake of Eden is the cause of civilization, Hudson's anthropomorphized snake is its victim:

Looking at a serpent of this kind, and I have looked at many a one, the fancy is born in me that I am regarding what was once a fellow-being, perhaps one of those cruel desperate wretches I have encountered on the outskirts of civilization, who for his crimes has been changed into the serpent form, and cursed with immortality. (26)

This serpent-vision of Hudson's will reappear in "Snake," a poem written by Hudson's avid reader, D. H. Lawrence. Both writers' empathy for the serpent signals the fact that the way back to Eden is the way of regression, "a revelation of an unfamiliar and un-suspected nature hidden under the nature we are conscious of," which Hudson attributes to "an instantaneous reversion to the primitive and wholly savage mental conditions" (200). The paradise that has been lost is, for Hudson, the lost happiness of childhood animality: "The return to an instinctive or primitive state of mind is accom-panied by this feeling of elation, which, in the very young, rises to an intense gladness, and sometimes makes them mad with joy, like animals newly escaped from captivity" (205). Here is the same "mad carousal" which Hardy's Mrs. Yeobright saw in the "wild ephemer-ons"; and years later Hudson would create, in Rima, an incarnation of the dream of the child-animal of freedom.

Naturism was related to the broad *fin-de-siècle* aesthetic move-ment known as primitivism. Gauguin's return to Tahiti in 1895 symbolized the primitivist impulse: seeking to escape the rationalism and dogmatism of his own culture, Gauguin discovered among the Tahitian natives a quality akin to the innocence of childhood. Hudson and Tomlinson located a similar aboriginal Eden in the jungle country of South America. It seemed indeed that Jean-Jacques Rousseau's ideal of "the noble savage" had come alive historically. The naturist movement is synchronous with the high-point of primitivism among painters from Gauguin and Henri Rousseau to the "Negro" periods of Vlaminck and Picasso.

Most of the naturists had read or been affected by Sir James Frazer's monumental and pioneering study of primitive societies, *The Golden Bough*, the first volume of which appeared in 1890, the last in 1915. Although Frazer himself was hardly free of imperial patronism toward "lesser breeds without the law," his treatise was part of a general reappraisal of "barbarian" cultures, and raised the question whether within the symbolic life of such cultures might be hidden a wisdom which the European white man had lost. Artists benefited immensely from the rapid growth of cultural anthropology – one of several new fields of social study based on Darwinism – for it suggested new subjects and new artistic styles. Most of the major painters and sculptors of the period – Gauguin, Rousseau, Van Gogh, Toulouse-Lautrec, Degas, Matisse, Vlaminck, Brancusi, Picasso – derived new shapes and colors from primitive artifacts and customs. *Ut pictura poesis:* the subject matter, the language, and the quality of description in naturist travel books and novels was, as we shall see, deeply indebted to the work of Frazer and his colleagues.

Naturism and primitivism alike reflected Darwin's (and anticipated Freud's) concern with the "unknown" within human nature in all places and times. But while there were primitivistic elements in naturism, the two movements were radically opposed in aesthetic practice. Where the primitivist typically seeks to reduce and distort nature into stylized abstract forms, the naturist prefers a realistic art of description; where the primitivist painter contracts space into the two-dimensional surface of his canvas, the naturist writer (with few exceptions) prefers the old-fashioned perspective of Renaissance-inspired art. Primitivism leads directly from Cézanne towards cubism; but for the naturists, this primordial formalism constituted a rejection of the claims of nature in favor of totemism. In *Women in Love*, Loerke's primitivist bronze statue of a young girl on a horse provides a representative example of the naturist distaste for this aspect of primitivism. Gudrun exclaims: "*Look* how stock and stupid and brutal it is. Horses are sensitive, quite delicate and sensitive, really." Loerke responds, after the manner of the moderns: ". . . that horse is a certain *form*, part of a whole form . . . it is part of a work of art, it has no relation to anything outside that work of art." And

Ursula then aptly summarizes the naturist objection to primitivism: "But why does he have this idea of a horse? I know it is his idea. I know it is a picture of himself, really – " (420–1). Forms are ideas; ideas are pictures of ourselves. The naturist seeks simplicity, but recognizes that to simplify is not to reduce or to formalize; it is rather to catch, from the living organism, a glimpse of the possibility which Thoreau tried to make actual at Walden: "Let us spend one day as deliberately as nature."

Hudson's *Idle Days* moves, then, from the paradise lost of civilization to the regained life of nature. "Civilized life," for Hudson, "is one of continual repression" (205), and the voyage to Patagonia is a movement toward "that feeling of relief, of escape, and absolute freedom which one experiences in a vast solitude, where man has perhaps never been, and has, at any rate, left no trace of his existence" (7).

Tomlinson's *The Sea and the Jungle* follows the same pattern: the writer's eyes, even in the midst of the Amazonian jungle, are upon civilized England, which for him is symbolized in the image of a printed page: England is "a population of bundles of newspapers" (165). Tomlinson's adventure begins, in fact, when he symbolically puts aside a book: "The waves were singing to themselves. A ray of light laughed in my eyes, playing hide and seek across the wisdom of my book. . . . I put the book down" (71). In *Idle Days*, Hudson had written, "I had cast aside the unread newspaper" (69); and Tomlinson appropriates the image: "I put down the papers with their calls to social righteousness pitched in the upper register of the tea tray" (10). Tomlinson's image recalls Butler's concluding sentence in *Alps and Sanctuaries*: "The science-ridden, art-ridden, culture-ridden, afternoon-tea-ridden cliffs of Old England rise upon the horizon" (275). Tomlinson's opposition between tea-tray and "waves singing to themselves" is also the imagery of T. S. Eliot's Prufrock who, among the coffee spoons, hears "mermaids singing each to each." For Tomlinson, in 1912, they sing; for Prufrock, in 1916, they do not. Eliot's Prufrock might well be taken to mark the beginning of the end of the naturist dream of Eden. Even Lawrence would at long last agree that "the hope of running our boat up a little creek and landing in the Garden of Eden" was an impossible dream: "This hope is always defeated. There is no Garden of Eden, and the Hesperides never were. . . . There are no happy lands" (*Phoenix*, 343).

Lawrence's recognition that there is no happy land does not alter the fact that he spent his life looking for it: his dream of Rananim, the colony he hoped to create with the Huxleys in Florida, remained a hope to the end. But Hudson and Tomlinson felt that they had found the "happy land" directly south of Rananim. Lawrence's remark serves to dramatize the vast difference between the naturists and their Christian humanist contemporaries, for whom Original Sin had destroyed forever all happy lands this side of heavenly paradise.

This difference is clearly illustrated in the contrast between Tomlinson's *The Sea and the Jungle* and Joseph Conrad's "The Heart of Darkness." A comparison between the two stories seems inevitable. Both are romantic tales of a journey up a river; both are expressions of a final vision of human nature. Conrad's story is fiction, Tomlinson's is not. Yet *The Sea and the Jungle*, both in its dramatic structure and its exotic mood, approaches the boundaries of romantic fiction. But where Marlowe's trip up the Congo is a voyage to "the dark places of the earth,"[10] Tomlinson's voyage up the Amazon is a journey toward light and life: "I felt instead that I could live and grow for ever in such a land" (187). In both cases the journey is a regression, a backward movement in time; but as Genesis approaches, Tomlinson's fascination is with the beauties of the Garden, Conrad's is with the terrors of the Serpent. "Going up that river," wrote Conrad, "was like travelling back to the earliest beginnings of the world, when vegetation rioted on the earth and the big trees were kings. An empty stream, a great silence, an impenetrable forest" (536). But where, for Conrad, "there was no joy in the brilliance of sunshine" (536), a similar intensity of light helps Tomlinson to see "the earth as a great and shining sphere" (129). Conrad comes to rest with the moment of Original Sin, while Tomlinson pauses at that pristine moment on the seventh day of rest and rejoicing, after the glories of nature had been freshly created: ". . . we looked upon what was there for the first time since Genesis, where we might have been in the hush of the seventh day. . . ." (203).

Tomlinson's careful description of landscape functions as part of a fiercely moral sensibility; his landscape is hardly less a *paysage moralisé* than Conrad's. But Tomlinson's faith of a naturalist allows him to dwell longer upon landscape, while Conrad's purpose is to transform, cast a spell, invest his landscape with a voodoo magic. In both cases, the jungle is a source of new knowledge, in the spirit of Darwin's remark about Patagonia: "Who would not look at these last boundaries to man's knowledge with deep but ill-defined sensations?"

Both stories provide the reader with a voyage of self-discovery. "The Heart of Darkness" represents a descent into the unconscious life of Marlowe whereby the inner core of his selfhood is revealed as isolated and irrevocably guilty. *The Sea and the Jungle* is equally an exploration of the unconscious; but here the self is identified with earth and physical nature, drawing strength and psychic health from an "ill-defined" bodily communion with sea and jungle and animal life. If Conrad's is a journey into exile, Tomlinson's is a voyage home.

Tomlinson's excursion into the regions of the unconscious involves the same lapse from rationality experienced by Darwin and Hudson. The process begins for Tomlinson as he watches the azure of sky and sea: "You feel your careless gaze snatched in the revolving hues speeding astern, and your consciousness is instantly unwound from your spinning brain, and you are left standing on the ship, an empty spool" (79–80). But this experience of the sea is merely preparatory to the experience of the jungle, which has a mind of its own: "It regards us with the vacancy of large composure, with a lofty watchfulness which has no need to show its mind. I think it knows our fears of its domain. It knows the secret of our fate. It makes no sign" (106). The primeval silence of the jungle prepares, in turn, for the stylized tableau – so like the Tahitian primitives of Gauguin – of the native women and children "negligent on the grass, sunning themselves" (111). They are described in terms of sunlight and animality; their movements are slow, or arrested, as if their bodies were free from the tyrannical pressures of mind and will: "They were as unconscious of their grace as animals. They looked round and up at us, and one stayed her hand, her comb half through the length of her hair . . ." (111).

Tomlinson's progress to this final vision of bodily integrity has been carefully prepared for. The trip across the sea was a process of unwinding the mind from the body; sensuous impressions of sea and sky have already won a victory over Tomlinson's brain. But the mind fights back; Tomlinson strains to fathom the meaning of the azure, and at last concludes that no meaning seems to be there: ". . . I can report no luck from my concentrated efforts on that symbol. The colour may have been its own reward" (76).

Color is of primary importance to the naturist travel book. Hudson is an especially vivid colorist; and D. H. Lawrence – especially in *Women in Love* – further refines the color symbolism which is apparent throughout Hudson's writing. Hudson's landscape is itself a

c

source of light, rather than a reflection of it. His plants and animals seem to burn with an intrinsic fire of vitality which is invariably portrayed in vivid primary hues. He notices, for example, "fully ripe cherries glowing like live coals amid the deep green foliage" (*Idle Days*, 16). This same foliage becomes the presiding spirit and the "principal personage" of Hudson's novel, *Green Mansions*.

The naturists move from the muted twilight greys and siennas of Egdon Heath into the bright morning light – the crimsons, yellows and greens – of southern and tropical lands. Hudson is quite conscious of his use of color; his clearest exposition of his color symbolism occurs midway in *Idle Days*, where he pauses to meditate on the passage in *Moby Dick* where Melville discusses "whiteness" and its effect on the mind. Like Melville, Hudson is taken with the "mystique" of whiteness: the fear it inspires in humans, the sense of primitive magic in the lack of color. But he rejects Melville's "supernatural" explanation and substitutes his own theory of "animism," "the mind's projection of itself into nature" (48).

In Hudson's work, this projection is never white; it is always prismatic, rainbow-colored. Hudson provides, both in theory and in practice, an interesting parallel to the school of French impressionists who are flourishing at the time of *Idle Days* (1893). Hudson is part of a broad movement in the arts to break away from nineteenth-century restraint in matters of color; and behind his continual use of a bright palette is a conscious and deliberate symbolism. One of the heavy costs of civilization, Hudson asserts, is our loss of visual power: we look, but we do not see. In a chapter of *Idle Days* entitled "Sight in Savages" (xi), he discusses this loss, and insists that "savages are our superiors in visual power" (157). More specifically, our "defective color-sense is due to the inimical conditions of our civilization" (158). The following chapter, "Concerning Eyes" (xii), is a discussion of this blurred color-sense in modern times. Hudson's landscapes are always bright; his eye falls immediately upon the most highly lighted parts of his picture. He sees, for example, a "magnetism" in a sunlit river, which has "the powerful effect of brightness, which fascinates us, as it does the moth, and the eye is drawn to it as to a path of shining silver" (45). The moth analogy is characteristic: Hudson instinctively strives to ennoble human nature by means of a bird or insect simile, in the spirit of Hardy.

It follows that Hudson is fascinated by rainbows: he finds himself wondering why "the Incas were the only worshippers of the rainbow" (49). For him it is the symbol of rejuvenation, of an "inward resurrection," for it possesses "a beauty that is not of the earth," a beauty that is transfigured. Hudson's symbol is appropriated by another worshipper who makes those same sunlit colors, "arching in the blood," the culminating image of his most ambitious novel. Hudson's fellow-worshipper is D. H. Lawrence; the novel, *The Rainbow*.

But Hudson's most searching experiments in symbolism are attempts to transcend the limits of human vision. The key to this search is his assertion that "sight, the most important of our senses, is the most intellectual" (219). The word "intellectual" for Hudson denotes a limitation as well as an excellence; and he looks to the qualities of touch, sound, and odor to convey a dimension of experience impenetrable to the eye alone. *Idle Days* ends with a chapter called "The Perfume of an Evening Primrose"; as Hudson writes the chapter, he holds a pen in one hand, a primrose in the other. His primrose, like Proust's madeleine soaked in tea, evokes "many scenes and events of the past." Yet the smell of the primrose has the effect for Hudson, as for Proust, of annihilating the past, of destroying time, by incorporating it in a glowing present: "I am no longer in an English garden recalling and consciously thinking about the vanished past, but during that brief moment time and space seem annihilated and the past is now" (218). Hudson's visionary moment with primrose and bird-song is not unlike the imagery T. S. Eliot will later use in his *Four Quartets*: the rose and lotus will replace Hudson's primrose; Eliot's bird, like Hudson's, will speak – "Go, go, go, said the bird" – and Eliot's past and future, like Hudson's, will "point to one end, which is always present."

Hudson's experience with the primrose leads him to a long passage of speculation upon the difference between the olfactory and the visual in human experience; he wonders about the fact that the visual can be recalled, and thus can attain a permanence in the memory, but fragrance is transitory and evanescent, and all the more beautiful for being so. It is precisely this transitory intensity which D. H. Lawrence seeks continually to evoke until, at the end of his life, the Bavarian gentian represents a final unity of life and death in the moment, and a final vision of the living beauty of darkness itself.[11]

Hudson's search for a non-visual symbolism led him, as an ornithologist, inevitably to what he calls "bird-music." In fact his only recorded complaint against Charles Darwin was that the great scientist wrote so little on the subject of bird-song (*Idle Days*, 144). For Hudson, the attraction of bird-song is that "there is no suggestion of human feeling in it" (137). It is a language unto itself, and cannot be represented in human words: "Bird music, and, indeed, bird sounds generally, are seldom describable" (135). This attempt to describe the undescribable, to employ language to evoke a meaningful pattern of sounds, is a characteristic preoccupation of naturist writers. Hudson's attempt to find in bird-song a symbol of the wisdom of nature – which culminates in the character of Rima, in *Green Mansions* – is a key link between Hardy's "language of nature" and Lawrence's continual search for a non-verbal and non-visual musical symbolism. For Lawrence will share Hudson's ornithological impression of man's genesis in Eden: "In the beginning," Lawrence will write in *Etruscan Places*, "was not a Word, but a chirrup" (53).

The chirrup which resounds from the pages of *Idle Days* and becomes the crucial experience for Abel in *Green Mansions* may be taken as a symbol of the continuity between the travel book and the naturist novel. This continuity extends beyond questions of theme to matters of narrative style, descriptive technique, characterization, and story structure. In these travel books, spirit of place provides a platform and a perspective from which a narrator can look from the outside toward modern England and, by extension, toward modern civilization. These writers, following Hardy, have developed a kind of landscape description which itself contains an implicit critique of civilized society. This critical mood reflects a new historical sophistication and a revived interest in comparative studies of culture: Nietzsche's insight into Greek civilization, Burckhardt's revolutionary study of the Italian Renaissance, and Frazer's compilation of primitive myths have prepared the way for *Idle Days*, *Old Calabria*, *The Sea and the Jungle*, and *Etruscan Places*.

This abandonment to spirit of place is essentially a literary means of probing into non-conceptual and instinctive areas of human experience. The loose structure of the travel book itself expresses the naturist revolt against the tyranny of concepts. The plot of the travel book is a sequence of impressions, often rationally unconnected. This revolt against the machine of deterministic cause-and-effect is symbolized by a rejection of clock time and an abandonment to the accidents of the present moment, the here and now. Thus the unbuttoned mood of *Alps and Sanctuaries* leads directly to the relaxed dilettantism of the last half of *The Way of All Flesh*; Douglas's pleasant days in Cosenza, "doing nothing whatever," prefigure *South Wind*; the impassioned geographical pursuit of the earth-life in *Sea and Sardinia* and *Etruscan Places* becomes a principle of story structure in *Aaron's Rod* and *Kangaroo*.

Idle Days and *The Sea and the Jungle* are constructed around a core of personal conversion: they build to and from moments of revelation. *Alps and Sanctuaries, Old Calabria,* and *Sea and Sardinia* are episodic, constructed around a series of momentary perceptions without any formal unity except the accidental unity of the journey itself. These moments of conversion become, in the naturist travel novel, the turning point of the plot: *South Wind* centers upon Bishop Heard's striking conversion to amorality as he accidentally witnesses a murder; *Where Angels Fear to Tread* is built around Lilia's romantic conversion in Monteriano; *The Lost Girl* rises to the moment when Alvina Houghton undergoes a spiritual rejuvenation in a desolate "Place called Califano"; *Green Mansions* builds slowly to Abel's revelatory vision of Rima.

Lawrence's travels have a profound effect upon the structure of his stories: after he begins his personal pilgrimage in 1915, his novels take on the *leitmotif* of place which characterizes *Women in Love, Aaron's Rod, Kangaroo,* and *The Plumed Serpent*. Aaron's journeys, for example, closely correspond to the movements of the first-person narrator in *Etruscan Places*.

These travelogues have provided an apprenticeship in landscape description; have created a new point of view identified with the genius of place; have brought to the novel a tradition of escape from mechanized time and industrialized place; have introduced a modern, Darwinian version of the myth of Eden. Lawrence gave the rallying cry for all naturist novelists, in his travelogue *Sea and Sardinia*: "Comes over one an absolute necessity to move. And what is more, to move in some particular direction. A double necessity, then: to get on the move, and to know whither" (1). The plot and the setting of the naturist novel was born out of the travel book.

4 Spirit of Place: The Novel

"The place has nothing to do with it at all," protests Mrs. Herriton in E. M. Forster's first novel, *Where Angels Fear to Tread* (1905).[1] Mrs. Herriton, puzzled by hints of a change that has come over her daughter in Italy, could not be more mistaken. The place – Monteriano – has everything to do not only with Lilia's development as a character, but with the theme and structure of the novel itself. The story is about spirit of place; it is a study of the effects of geography upon character; it is built around a dialogue between proper England and pagan Italy; its leading characters are travellers; its opening scene takes place in Charing Cross Station.

Where Angels Fear to Tread is representative of a new kind of novel which appeared in England at the turn of the century: the novel of travel. The earlier romantic travel tales of Robert Louis Stevenson or Rider Haggard can hardly be called novels, for they lack that "criticism of life" which from the beginning characterized the novel as a form. The new fiction is in fact closer to the spirit of the non-fiction travel book. Indeed, the distinction between the two genres is not always clear. What is certain is that there is a common impulse at work in both forms. Conrad's first novel (*Almayer's Folly*), Kipling's first stories, Hudson's and Cunninghame Graham's travel-fictions – all make their appearance in the years 1895–1900.

These first tales of Conrad and Kipling mark the beginning of a period of about twenty-five years during which spirit of distant place dominates English fiction. Hardy's local spirit of place, which lay like a silent brooding reminder of the conflict between the world of nature and the world of man in society, was essential to the mood of irony in his novels. In the new novel that conflict remains, but the irony tends to disappear as physical place begins to win a victory over civilized society. In this process of change, Conrad is transitional, for his stories project a final irony that relates him to Hardy. In *The Outcast of the Islands* (1896), *Lord Jim* (1900), and "The Heart of Darkness" (1902), strange and exotic climes represent both a hope and an ultimate disappointment: Conrad's outposts of civilization evoke, finally, a sense of exile and isolation. For both Conrad and his admirer Henry James, the "beast in the jungle" symbolizes a primitive evil which hides in the heart of human nature. Yet Conrad's express purpose, which is to "create the moral, the emotional atmosphere of the place and the time,"[2] is representative of the broad aims of the new travel novelist.

The jungle itself, for example, plays quite different but equally powerful roles in the stories of Conrad, Kipling, and Hudson. Kipling's *Jungle Books* (1894–5) provide, along with their sheer appeal as fantasy, an extraordinary blending of the exotic and the moral. Kipling's story of Mowgli among the animals can be seen as a kind of *Bildungsroman*, the adventure story of a boy's education-in-nature. To be sure, Kipling is far from recommending the law of the jungle over the law of human society; yet Mowgli's eventual return to the human world destroys neither the charm nor the fraternal lessons of the jungle world. Mowgli is a prototype of the new fictional hero, not in his return to society, but in his escape from it – and his escape is the substance of the book. As the boy who runs away, Mowgli prefigures Butler's Ernest Pontifex, Joyce's Stephen Dedalus, Lawrence's Paul Morel, Hudson's Abel, Douglas's Denis.

Both the *Jungle Books* and *Kim* (1901) are expressions of an impulse to fantasize about the attractiveness of the primitive, amoral life. Both Mowgli and Kim are evolutionary reversions: they both return to a relatively animal existence, with its dangers and its freedoms. Like Mowgli, Kim escapes from the world of civilized restraint to seek adventure in strange and exotic rural India. From the first words of the book – "He sat, in defiance of municipal orders, astride the gun Zam'Aammah" – we see Kim as a truant from the civilized world of the English school, and Kim weaves between one world and the other throughout the novel. *Kim* is built upon spirit of place; its hero mediates between East and West, India and England. The story relates Kim's physical movement, alongside his beloved lama; yet the lama's excitement comes from his anticipation of reaching his goal, where Kim's joy is in the movement, the adventure, itself.

Kipling's tendency to deal, in his fiction and his poetry, with "two separate sides to my head" – with both the civilized Englishman and the frontier adventurer – is also typical of Forster's novels, from *Where Angels* to *A Passage to India* (1924). There is a special geographical dialectic in each Forster novel: Monteriano, in *Where Angels*, and Florence, in *A Room with a View*, carry on ineffective dialogues with London; in *Howards End*, the opposition between city apartment and country seat is the focus of several dualities – culture against business, lower against upper middle-class, sexual love against "decency." In *The Longest Journey*, the pagan ruins at Cadbury Range play against the student world at Cambridge; and *A Passage to India* resumes Kipling's halting dialogue between East and West.

Yet Kipling's psychology of place enters into Forster's fiction through other authors as well. Fresh in Forster's mind as he commenced his first novel was his reading of Henry James's *The Ambassadors*, published in 1903. James's Lambert Strether, sent on a mission to Paris from the tightly puritanical New England business town of Woollett, discovers, along with the relaxed charm of Paris, a new liberation of the mind and the sensibility. This pattern of liberation through change of place is the theme of *Where Angels*: the novel is a dialogue between climates, the Mediterranean against the Nordic. The theme is set at the beginning: "No one realized that more than strong personalities were engaged; that the struggle was national; that generations of ancestors, good, bad or indifferent, forbad the Latin man to be chivalrous to the northern woman, the northern woman to forgive the Latin man" (65).

Norman Douglas develops this climatic theme in *South Wind*, paying more specific attention to the physical effect of warm air, the chemical action of sunlight upon the northern temperament: "Northern minds seem to become fluid here, impressionable, unstable, unbalanced – what you please. There is something in the brightness of this spot which decomposes their old particles and arranges them into fresh and unexpected patterns" (150). By the time of *Aaron's Rod* (1922) and *The Plumed Serpent* (1926), the climatic theme has attained the status of a literary platitude, not only in the novel, but in every form of writing. For example, Synge's report of his visit to the Aran Islands in 1898, along with his *Riders to the Sea* (1904), provides an eloquent testimony to that same search for roots in the soil which is the subject of our inquiry. Indeed the Gaelic revival itself is a symptom of the new importance of spirit of place: from Innisfree to Coole to the stately tower of his later poems, place dominates the poetry of Yeats, as it dominates his plays.

This new sense of physical place is confined neither to a single genre nor to a single national literature. On the continent, André Gide's *Fruits of the Earth* (1897) projects, in a series of Nietzschean aphorisms, the narrator's excited discovery of the nourishing power of the soil. Both Gide and Thomas Mann are preoccupied, especially in their early writing, with the dialectic of climate: North Africa for the Gide of *The Immoralist* (1902) or *If It Die* (1926), and Italy for the Thomas Mann of "Tonio Kroger" (1903), symbolize a sensual release which contrasts with the inhibited, intellectual Nordic temperament. Gide's *Urien's Voyage* (1893) parallels the river pilgrimages of Conrad and Tomlinson; Mann's *The Magic Mountain* (1924) provides a topographical symbolism which echoes the enchanted snow-capped peaks of naturist literature, from Butler's Alps to those of Lawrence in *Women in Love*.

Within the first few years of the new century, the travel novel is firmly established as a tradition. Even Arnold Bennett's *The Old Wives' Tale* (1908), a realistic study of English provincial and commercial life, is constructed around Sophia's flight to Paris and her adventures there. Sophia – like Mowgli and Kim – returns to England, but Bennett's portrait of the Five Towns is given clarity and force by the Parisian perspective which occupies the central sections of the novel. Like Sophia, H. G. Wells's Mr. Polly (1910) rebels and takes to the road; and although Polly stays in England, he finds a new "home" which Wells clearly intends to be as exciting as Kim's India or Abel's Brazil. Polly's departure from wife and shop is a scene which is repeated constantly in the fiction of the second decade. R. B. Cunninghame Graham's novels are typical in this respect: *Brought Forward* (1917), for example, begins with a characteristic sentence: "The workshop in Parkhead was not inspiring"; and in chapter two we quite naturally find our hero on the banks of the Uruguay River.

During these years spirit of place enters into almost every important piece of fiction. Conrad's *Under Western Eyes* (1911), as its title suggests, is a study in contrast between East and West Europe; Joyce's *Dubliners* (1914) is held together by a unity of place which reflects a barrenness and conformity of mind; Douglas's *South Wind* attains a tenuous unity through spirit of place alone. Lawrence's *Sons and Lovers* (1913) and Joyce's *A Portrait of the Artist as a Young Man* (1916) build toward permanent departures, permanent exile in foreign lands. The year 1922, which marks the limits of our inquiry, saw four important works published, all of which are deeply concerned with spirit of place: Joyce's *Ulysses*, constructed upon an elaborate symbolism of parallel location; T. E. Lawrence's *Seven Pillars of Wisdom*, recounting his ambivalent love affair with Arabia; D. H. Lawrence's *Aaron's Rod*, partly novel and partly travel book, but always concerned with education-by-tourism; and finally, T. S. Eliot's *The Waste Land*, whose early sections documenting the decline of the West are answered, in measure, by the voice of Eastern spirituality in the triune formula of the *Upanishads*.

This rapid survey is sufficient to indicate that the new fiction is built upon a new relationship between character and place. In these novels geography becomes, like the medieval maps of love, an emblem of psychology; the travel hero glosses the landscape for directional signals; his movement across the face of the earth becomes the key element in plot structure. We are reminded of the moving figures in the Hardy novels; yet our recognition of the continuity between Hardy and the new novelists, in regard to spirit of place, carries with it a firm qualification. The places themselves are quite different from Hardy's, and they are used for new effects. Hardy's spirit of place involves a single, fixed location, a landscape that surrounds and supports the characters. Hardy's humans move across the landscape like flies across an ancient rock, and in their movement is both their aspiration and their doom. The new novel, on the contrary, evokes spirit of place in terms of two locations, representing two states of mind or ways of life. The purpose of the leading character is to move from one location to another; the plot represents his difficulty – physically and psychologically – in doing so; the texture and pace of the new story is determined by an antiphony of place. Hardy's "President of the Immortals," no longer capriciously cruel, has disappeared into the jungle, or into a small Italian village, or on to an escarpment in the Alps, where he awaits the hero with a smile and open arms.

The new novel, like the travel literature upon which it is patterned, tells the story of a movement from the tight enclosures of England to the freedom of a kind of frontier world of nature. Kim, Strether, Lilia, Polly, Paul Morel, Stephen Dedalus – each in his own way is seeking liberation through change of place. The naturist novel, then, contains two basic elements: (a) the story of entrapment – by family, Christian morality, commercialism – expressed in the tightly-plotted reportorial style of the social realist, and (b) the story of liberation – geographical and spiritual – embodied in a loosely woven plot and a relaxed style which closely resembles the form of pastoral romance. The problem of the naturist novelist was to create a unified work of the imagination out of these two contrasting elements. My purpose here is to describe how they went about solving this problem.

For these two elements of the story, two novels tended to serve as models. Both were highly esteemed during the first two decades of the twentieth century; both were widely imitated by practicing novelists. The classic model for the story of entrapment was Butler's *The Way of All Flesh*, first published posthumously in 1903; the fictional model for the story of liberation was Hudson's *Green Mansions* (1904), a book whose enormous popularity (which declined sharply, along with Hudson's, after the First World War) is an important barometer of Edwardian taste.

The naturist story of the trapped hero is the story of the family, as the original title of Butler's novel indicates: "Ernest Pontifex or The way of all Flesh – a story of English Domestic life."[3] It is a title which might apply with equal validity to Hardy's *Jude the Obscure*; and the tragedy of little Father Time, so briefly handled by Hardy, is not unlike the more detailed and penetrating story of Ernest Pontifex. This similarity of theme serves to emphasize the vast difference between the two novels. Where Hardy's story is structured on principles of architecture or geometry, the structure of Butler's novel derives from principles of biology.

Ernest Pontifex is an embryo; his story is told as a series of causal relationships, each phase illustrating the action of the environment upon a developing child organism. Butler's artistic success in the first sections of the novel – as distinct from his failure in the latter sections – is a direct result of his ability to find a psychological analogy to the processes of evolutionary biology:

> Embryo minds, like embryo bodies, pass through a number of strange metamorphoses before they adopt their final shape. It is no more to be wondered at that one who is going to turn out a Roman Catholic should have passed through the stages of being first a free thinker, than that a man should at some former time have been a mere cell, and later on an invertebrate animal. Ernest however could not be expected to know this. Embryos never do. (33).

But the development of Ernest Pontifex, embryo mind, is at every stage a betrayal of Ernest Pontifex, embryo body, for the Pontifex parents seem determined to suppress, in the name of Christian morality, his every animal impulse. Pontifex family life has one overriding purpose: to kill the animal, and to create a "Father Time" whose only grasp of reality comes through moral abstractions. What the Pontifex parents actually create is, of course, a neurotic; and in this fact lies the paradox of *The Way of All Flesh*. For neurosis is by its very nature an organic failure, a malfunction. Thus from the moment that Ernest achieves manhood and independence from his family, Butler's novel begins to disintegrate structurally. Hardy was the more proficient novelist: he disposed of Father Time, along with the brothers and sisters, in a gruesome but efficient multiple murder–suicide. Butler, on the other hand, tries to complete his story of entrapment with a sequel of liberation; but his subject matter is no longer amenable to a style based upon biological analogy. Ernest, the embryo mind, has developed; Ernest, the embyro animal, is forever maimed. In his treatise, *Life and Habit*, Butler the biologist emphasized the immutability of this process whereby the emotional pattern becomes fixed early in life. But Butler the novelist is reduced to the tired cliché of endowing his hero with a material fortune and thus, presumably, with happiness.

This failure of the last part of Butler's novel provides, however, a key to naturist fiction, for the new novelists are concerned to provide a "second half" to the new kind of *Bildungsroman* of which Butler's story is the beginning. Forster's establishment England, so strongly modelled on the world of father Pontifex, has a counterpoint in Florence or Monteriano; Lawrence contrasts Paul Morel's family misery with his quiet moments with flowers, a sketch-book, and, above all, Clara. Joyce's Stephen Dedalus, entrapped by family, nation, and religion, has counterpointing epiphanies with poems and songs and school friends; Wells's Polly leaves his wife to find a cloak-and-dagger world which provides a more unified, if less probable, adventure of liberation than that of Ernest. Abel finds Rima; Aaron discovers Lilly; Lady Chatterley falls into the arms of a willing gamekeeper. All begin, in one manner or another, in the family trap experienced by Ernest Pontifex. But one of the primary challenges to the new novelist was to discover techniques by means of which a hero's liberation and rebirth into the physical life could be embodied. Butler, writing in the 1870s, had not yet hit upon the novelistic answer which the naturists eventually borrowed from Hardy: to symbolize the search for animality through spirit of place. Yet if we take Butler's later writings as sequels to his autobiographical novel, the spirit of place that dominates *Alps and Sanctuaries* indicates that he was looking in the same direction as the later novelists.

To be sure, in *The Way of All Flesh* Butler created several brief and disconnected episodes to represent Ernest's struggle to recover his animality. The most representative scene is the one in which a cure is prescribed for Ernest's "sickness"; he is ordered by his doctor to visit a zoo:

> I have found the Zoological Gardens of service to many of my patients. I should prescribe for Mr. Pontifex a course of the larger mammals. Don't let him think he is taking them medicinally, but let him go to their house twice a week for a fortnight and stay with the hippopotamus, the rhinoceros, and the elephants, till they begin to bore him. I find these beasts do my patients more good than any others. (307)

This prescribed nostrum of larger mammals seems to work, and Ernest's appetite improves. But Butler's cerebral manner of concluding the episode leaves the reader unconvinced about the magical effect of jungle lure upon Ernest: "I found the doctor quite right in his estimates of the larger mammals as the ones which on the whole were most beneficial, and observed that Ernest . . . seemed to be drinking in large draughts of their lives to the re-creation and regeneration of his own" (308). Butler's Zoological Gardens, in one manifestation or another, reappear continually in twentieth-century literature, from Old Jolyon's refreshing visit to the zoo in Galsworthy's *The Man of Property* to Jerry's communion with the Central Park animals in *The Zoo Story*; and in each case the zoo represents this same struggle for a re-creation and regeneration of the instinctual life. Hardy's treatment of animal life had signalled a renewal of interest in man's animality; but Kipling's *Jungle Tales*, by means of a single artistic focus on the animal world, furnished the naturists with an unforgettably powerful image of the dangerous beauty of animal life, and of its relevance to human wisdom.

At the time of Kipling's *Jungle Books*, H. G. Wells published a science-fantasy entitled *The Island of Doctor Moreau*. Moreau creates a series of metamorphoses by means of vivisection, and his quasi-human creatures are intended by Wells to remind his readers of the horrors of animality lurking beneath the tenuous rationality of humans. Yet the final horror of the story comes from the satanic scientism of Moreau; the reader is inclined to pity the animals whose natural dignity and integrity has been so cruelly destroyed. Wells's story, like Kipling's animal tales, reminds us of the close link between the beast in the jungle and man's own animal nature.

Yet these stories by Kipling and Wells are essentially entertainments, and it is not my purpose to gloss them for meanings, but merely to cite them as symptomatic of a revival of interest in the mystery of man's animality. This new interest has a profound effect upon fictional characterization, following Hardy's lead. Thus Forster's Gino and Lawrence's Cicio are presented largely in terms of a smooth animal agility; thus Mr. Polly "was particularly charmed by ducklings."[4] Rabbits, dead and alive, populate Lawrence's *The White Peacock*, to be replaced in his later fiction by horses, serpents, and foxes; and *South Wind* begins with a characteristic reference to the Bishop's "sneaking fondness for the natives – they were such fine, healthy animals" (1).

For the new novelists – Forster, Wells, Douglas, Lawrence, Joyce – Ernest Pontifex as embryo mind provides an unforgettable and highly imitable model. But for the new generation of writers, Ernest's visits to the zoo remain an unsatisfactory artistic means of telling the story of liberation. A year after the publication of *The Way of All Flesh*, W. H. Hudson created a character named Abel, who has only contempt for citified zoological gardens. Abel follows the animals to their native habitat, Kipling's jungle. He discovers there a law of the jungle quite different from Kipling's; for "in that wood there is one law, the law that Rima imposes, and outside of it a different law."[5] Abel loves a bird-girl whose beauty contrasts sharply with Wells's grotesque ape-men, a girl who echoes Hardy's bird-girl, Tess. Abel is a novelistic brother to the inveterate voyager of the travel literature of Doughty, Butler, Darwin, and Hudson himself; without Hudson's travelogues, there could have been no Abel. Hudson's *Green Mansions* (1904) represents a central turning-point in the progress of naturism from Hardy to Lawrence.

" 'The snake has bitten me,' I said. 'What shall I do? Is there no leaf, no root you know that would save me from death? Help me! Help me!' I cried in despair" (83). This *de profundis*, chanted by the hero of *Green Mansions*, suggests both the setting and the form of the novel. The scene is Eden; the form, a pastoral epic in prose. The hero, Abel, recalls the pastoral shepherd, victim of the first crime after the Fall. Yet Hudson's Abel lacks the innocence of the Renaissance pastoral hero: Abel has been bitten by the snake of civilization. Out of the Babylon of Caracas he emerges, seeking the promised land; but again and again he loses his way in the dense black wood. We are reminded of the despairing cries at the beginning of *Idle Days*: " 'We are lost,' I heard one say; and another answer, 'Aye, lost for ever!' " (2). These are words Dante often heard in the Inferno; and Abel's "dense black wood" inevitably recalls Dante's "selva oscura." Indeed, Abel's words often seem a paraphrase of the opening lines from the "Inferno": "I soon became entangled in a dense undergrowth, which so confused me that at last I confessed despairingly to myself that for the first time in this wood I was hopelessly lost" (84). Like Dante, Abel is led into paradise by a lady's voice; like Dante's great comedy, Hudson's novel is a chart of that journey. The latitudes of Dante's universe are degrees between Heaven and Hell; Hudson's latitudes measure the distance between civilized Caracas and primitive Orinoco. Like Dante, Abel is himself an enthusiastic map-maker: he constructs on a Guayanian plain a huge map of South America and the world in order to give Rima a geography lesson (146). But the lesson is not without irony, for it is Abel, not Rima, who is lost, and his geography tutorial, which opens Rima's eyes to the vast lands and seas beyond her lair, is the beginning of her destruction.

Abel knows that Rima dwells like Beatrice at the center where he will find his true self. Thus Abel's oft-repeated question, "Where am I?" is simultaneously the question, "Who am I?" For in *Green Mansions*, place begets identity. Rima symbolizes place; Abel finds his location when he finds Rima. And Rima's answer, like Beatrice's, is the only possible one: "I am here; now you know where you are." Hudson's story, in the allegorical tradition of Dante, Spenser, and Bunyan, conveys a spiritual adventure through a language of place. In *Green Mansions*, place represents man's longing to recover the integrity of his animal and instinctual life.

Hudson's subject, like Dante's and Bunyan's, is salvation: "I had allowed," Abel laments, "my only chance of salvation to slip by" (84). Abel had failed to listen to the only directional signal on the voyage to salvation: the voice of Rima. Rima's song is itself the spirit of Eden. Rima, the bird-girl, like the Christian *spiritus sanctus* – third person of the Trinity, represented always in the figure of a bird – is the breath and voice of a truth which transcends words because the truth is itself a place: paradise, Eden, Orinoco.

Green Mansions is written in the first person; yet Abel's point of view is eccentric, peripheral: he is trying to see life from Rima's point of view. It is her vision, not Abel's, that is the focal point of the novel; and Rima, in turn, embodies a spirit of place. Hudson, then, is feeling his way toward establishing place as a point of view. Hardy, once again, has anticipated Hudson: his Egdon Heath "watches . . . silent and intent," and registers all the transitory actions of the humans who walk upon it. Hudson, developing Hardy's insight, will pass on to the naturists a new objective in fiction: the aim of representing a point of view outside man's consciousness, a view-point from within the sub-human world.

Hudson's method is not allegory; his Rima is not a bird by the license of metaphor alone; his paradise is not, like Dante's mystical rose, a choir of disembodied souls. Hudson's Eden, like Kipling's jungle, is a land of real animals whose native beauty has not been "sicklied o'er with the pale cast of thought": "Why had Nature not done this before – why in all others does the brightness of the mind dim that beautiful physical brightness which the wild animals have?" (80). Abel encounters Rima as part of the animal world, and gradually this world of physical organism becomes for Abel existence itself: " – I called it being, not bird, now – "(40). Abel, in his litany of praise to Rima, associates her with the whole evolutionary range of organic life:

> Listen, Rima, you are like all beautiful things in the wood – flower, and bird, and butterfly, and green leaf, and frond, and little silky-haired monkey high up in the trees. . . . And when I listen to Rima's voice, talking in a language I cannot understand, I hear the wind whispering in the leaves . . . (113).

Abel of course falls in love with Rima, but Hudson holds firmly to standards of propriety, and *Green Mansions* remains a triumph of sexual sublimation. Rima is a direct descendant of the ladies of courtly love: inspiring but frigid. Yet Hudson's association of animalism with femininity marks a major step towards the earth-mother eroticism of Lawrence. If Rima totally lacks the buxom sexuality of some of Lawrence's heroines, she resembles them in her closeness to the rhythms of organic life. During the years 1908–10 young Lawrence read Hudson's articles in the *English Review* with avid interest, and spoke of Hudson's *South American Sketches* as "a wonderful find."[6] Of all the naturist writers, Hardy, Hudson, and Lawrence are closest to the spirit of primitivism; and Hudson is the immediate source, along with Hardy, of Lawrence's primitivism. Luminous descriptions of flowers, birds, and animals are frequent in *Green Mansions*, as they are in the stories of Lawrence. Both writers frame their plots around a pair of lovers; Lawrence's Paul escapes like Abel from house to woods, looking for a Rima. It is no surprise that Hudson, one of the first readers of *Sons and Lovers*, found it to be "a very good book indeeed."[7]

Hardy had removed the traditional setting of the Victorian novel from the drawing-room into the open air of fields and woods, creating a kind of pastoral tragedy in prose. Hudson continued both Hardy's pastoral setting and his sad ending, but with a vast difference. Though Rima dies, the final effect of Hudson's tale is not tragic: the reader remembers, not Rima's death, but Abel's romance. This change of emphasis is crucial.

The development of the English novel in the two decades following *Jude the Obscure* is in large part the story of the assimilation of romantic elements into a genre whose traditional virtues had been those of verisimilitude and a sense of the ordinary. Elements of the romanesque – the fanciful, extravagant, or supernatural – had appeared in the prose tales of Stevenson, Haggard, and Wilde. One of Conrad's contributions, in his early tales, was to integrate the mood of exotic romance with a psychological realism.

Green Mansions reflects a broad tendency to utilize elements of pastoral romance to tell the story of liberation. If Hudson's Abel is a city boy from Caracas, his name evokes the shepherd slain by his brother Cain. His name represents a hope, an aspiration to return to an Eden among the animals. Abel is cut in the pattern of Clym Yeobright, who returns from the corruptions of Paris to the rural life. Abel is a cousin to Jude Fawley, for though Jude aspires to the city and to culture while Abel longs for the jungle, the reader has no doubt that Jude's only happiness remains behind him in the country, among the birds he refuses, as scarecrow, to frighten away.

Hudson's Abel is a modern version of Spenser's Colin Clout, and Rima is a naturist Faerie Queene. *Green Mansions* revives both the mood and the structure of Spenser's great pastoral epic. Both works are blends of social criticism and rural romance; both evoke a nostalgia for the lost Eden, a nostalgia often reflected in stylistic archaism, just as Doughty's linguistic archaism relates to his preoccupation with a lost paradise. Both *Green Mansions* and *The Faerie Queene* tell stories of shepherds who meditate sadly upon the corruption of city life, and who search for a lady who will bring salvation through love; both involve plots based upon an endless wandering in a green world, a becoming lost and found and lost again. Both works represent a relaxing of the formal pressures of plot unity, an episodic freedom, a delight in digression; for in both, plot follows the accidental variations of landscape as the hero moves across it; in both, plot has the *non-sequitur* quality of accidental encounter. Landscape in both is a source of plot, and the reader has the feeling that there is no beginning or end, that the plot represents a continuous process. There is a loss of suspense, but there is also a new quality of intensity.

Hudson's most significant contribution to naturist fiction, and to Lawrence in particular, was his recasting of the pastoral novel of Hardy. Hardy's woodlanders are forever English; Hudson moves his woodlanders out of England into a brave new world. Hardy's stories are pervaded by a mood of impending catastrophe, Hudson's by a mood of idyll. Hardy's poetry of organism plays ironically against his geometry of doom; Hudson's botanical imagery dominates his fragile plot. Hardy's reader is left with an image of darkness, Hudson's with an image of light. Hardy's characters move physically at cross purposes within a confined circle; Hudson's Abel reaches his destination. In each respect, *Green Mansions* constitutes an important link between the novels of Hardy and those of Lawrence.

The novels of Dickens, Thackeray, and George Eliot were written from a point of view within society. The Edwardian establishes a central point of view outside the community of English life. In the service of this new critical spirit, the romantic tale plays a large part. The re-introduction of melioristic and romantic elements into the English novel at the turn of the century heralds a new spirit of social criticism, and sharply distinguishes the new romance from that of Stevenson or Haggard. The new romance is a conscious search for new roots, personal and communal, in the natural world.

Once again Hardy is the key: his novels are orchestrated with exotic and romantic strains. Hardy's character-names are themselves indicative: Bathsheba, Sergeant Troy, Wildeve, d'Urberville. But exotic romance in Hardy plays against the sordid and tragic tyranny of society over the individual: the evocative silhouette of Stonehenge in the closing scene of *Tess* is typical of Hardy's use of romance to heighten pathos. In Hardy's novels romantic threads are woven into the plot but remain subordinate to his larger tragic themes; but in the new novel, these strains of romance become principles of plot structure.

Thus Forster's Italy is a land of romance for his English heroines, and it is these same romantic elements – the relaxed morality, the pagan sexuality, the animal vitality – which provide a platform for the novelist's critique of English upper-middle-class propriety. In like manner, H. G. Wells, though he professes to be anti-romantic, utilizes romance for a specifically social purpose: his wildly romantic hero, Mr. Polly, is drawn entirely in terms of the society against which he rebels; without his drab lower-middle-class background, Polly would lose all his fictional force. The romance of Polly is centered in the words *"you can change it"*; the world, which has been Polly's tormentor, becomes, through romance, his oyster.

Polly's discovery serves to emphasize a vital difference between the philosophy of the naturists and the earlier primitivism of Rousseau and the romantics. The action of escape in the naturist novel is a parable of social change, and the naturist search for Eden reaches essentially into the future rather than the past, just as Wells's time machine moves always forward in time. For Polly's discovery that "if the world does not please you, *you can change it*" (172) is a culminating statement of the meliorism we have traced through Butler, Hardy, and the Edwardians. Polly's triumphant cry is not only a theme of naturist fiction, it is also a clue to the structure of the naturist novel. During the same years that George Bernard Shaw was turning the well-made Victorian melodrama upside down in order to make it an instrument of social criticism, the new novelists were utilizing the structural principles of pastoral romance for a similar purpose.

Hardy's tightly constructed plots came at the end of a century dominated by the spectre of determinism – evolutionary, historical, social, and economic. The ineluctable mechanism of Hardy's plots suggests the power of environment over men's lives; yet the meliorism reflected in Hardy's last two novels was bound eventually to be mirrored in the structure of the English novel. The plots of *Tess* and *Jude* are no less fatalistic than those of Hardy's earlier works; he merely shifts his emphasis from the determinism of the gods to the determinism of social prejudices. To the very end, Hardy's novels are stories of entrapment. Yet Hardy is at pains to let his reader know that this process is fabricated in large part by man's own folly.

For Hardy, fate is manifested as cruel caprice; as a plot technique this caprice is manifested as coincidence. The social attitudes which destroy Tess and Jude have neither law nor logic to support them: the ultimate cause of human misery is "crass casualty," or "hap." By "casualty" Hardy means the opposite of "causality"; and it is upon this very opposition between similar words that Hardy's irony ultimately depends. Thus Hardy's rebellion against "logic" or "rationality" plays ironically against the tight inevitability of his plot structures.

Samuel Butler too rebels vigorously against Darwinian determinism; like Emerson and Whitman, Butler is fond of inconsistency. His Ernest Pontifex recommends it as a primary rule of faith: "Then he saw that it matters little what profession, whether of religion or irreligion, a man may make, provided only he follows it out with charitable inconsistency" (*Way*, 260). Butler's model for the faithful was not Saint Paul. It was the Church of Laodicea, where "each individual member should only be hot in striving to be as lukewarm as possible" (343). And the story of the liberation of Ernest Pontifex, after he leaves the clutches of his family, is the story of his spirited reaction against the importance of being earnest. He becomes a model of capriciousness, as Butler himself had done.

This mood of freedom and abandon was repeated in all the writings of Norman Douglas. For contemporary readers, whose critical tastes have been formed in the age of the "new criticism," the structural carelessness of a novel like *South Wind* constitutes a fatal flaw. But the naturist saw differently: Tomlinson characterized Douglas's descriptive technique as one of "careless exactitude,"[8] and it was the highest compliment Tomlinson could offer. Tomlinson viewed this charm of the adventitious in Douglas's works as a valid principle of style: "Is learning that when it is merry? Is a prose style seriously fraught when it skips and flies? Perhaps, despite Sterne's assistance, we have not yet worked sufficiently free from the Augustan tradition. Great Gibbon never skipped, nor does Mr. Santayana" (*Douglas*, 14). Tomlinson was speaking of *Old Calabria*, and comparing it with Sterne's *A Sentimental Journey*; yet his argument might extend as well to *South Wind* and *Tristram Shandy*. For Sterne, like Butler and Douglas, was not only reacting against a tyranny of literary form, he was also asserting the rights of caprice as against the domination of logic. Sterne and Douglas were following Samuel Butler's prescription: "A man had better follow his instinct than attempt to decide . . . by any means of reasoning" (*Way*, 246).

Just as Sterne was reacting against the mechanical ticking of the Newtonian watch, so Butler and Douglas were rebelling against the deterministic implications of evolutionary theory. This devotion to the capricious and accidental is reflected in all naturist fiction, and in each novelist it assumes a different form. It is especially notable in Kipling's fiction. Kim is a truant from responsibility; he is simply playing the Great Game. The precondition of the game is freedom from social duties and moral truths. Kim's adventures in the high politics and espionage of empire have to do neither with England's glory, nor with justice, nor with truth. Kim is a boy; he is having fun. He is a creature of pure caprice.

An analogous impulse is displayed by H. G. Wells in his early novels. Wells likes to endow his characters with bizarre, absurd, or eccentric qualities, somewhat in the manner of Dickens. Polly's independence, for example, is illustrated by the absurdity of his conversations with the plump woman, by the strange tastes he acquires, by the mock-epic quality of his war with Uncle Jim, or by his affair with the eggs. Similar devices appear in *Tono-Bungay*: the absurd balloon ride, or the affair of the "quap," convey this same mood of caprice.

Forster's practice of punctuating his carefully made plots with gratuitous reversals is a manifestation of this same urge. The suddenness of the revelation of Lilia's marriage (*Where Angels*, 38), or of Helen's seduction by Leonard Bast,[9] like the totally unprepared-for deaths of Gerald,[10] Lilia (*Where Angels*, 68), or Mrs. Moore,[11] provide moments of surprise and suspense, but they also relate to Forster's interest in discontinuity. These sudden turns break into Forster's setting of genteel rationality with the efficiency of an axe; they remind us of Forster's preoccupation with the absurdities of existence.

This Edwardian search for a gratuitous or sub-rational narrative sequence is part of the same artistic impulse which gave rise to the technique known as "stream of consciousness." The flow of associations which emerges from the characters of James Joyce and Virginia Woolf, the "free association" sequences of the naturist novel, the *"inconséquences"* of Gide's novels, and the "surrealism" of the graphic artist during these same years — all are part of the same broad movement in the arts to discover ways of expressing that dimension of human experience which is independent of logical or causal connections.

The development of Lawrence as a novelist is in large part the account of his continued effort to embody this same reaction against a death-dealing causality. The Newtonian time-mechanism and the Baconian cause-mechanism are symbols of death in Lawrence's stories, while careless surrender to the moment always represents release and vitality. This duality lies at the core of the naturist novel; it is one of many indications of Hardy's continuing influence on Edwardian fiction.

For the spirit of Thomas Hardy dominates the naturist novel. Jude Fawley, for example, stands at the beginning of a succession of naturist characters. When Wells sees in Jude "the voice of the educated proletarian, speaking more distinctly than it has ever spoken before in English literature,"[12] he might also be thinking of his own

Mr. Polly, or of Forster's Leonard Bast who struggles to learn about
Beethoven, or about Lawrence's Paul Morel, the coal miner's son who
sketches, or about George Saxton, farmer-turned-innkeeper. Jude's
child, Father Time, reappears in the babies produced by fateful
unions of Lilia and Gino, or Helen and Leonard Bast. The sexual
themes treated by Hardy in *Tess* and *Jude* become explicit and central
in Forster and, partly through Forster's influence, in Lawrence.

This line of influence from Hardy through Forster to Lawrence
can be clearly seen by comparing *Where Angels Fear to Tread* with
The Lost Girl (1920). In both novels an inhibited conventional
English girl is sexually attracted to a young Italian; in both, they are
married and live in Italy. Each novel studies the struggle between
social convention and sexual attraction; each conveys the shock the
girl experiences in making the transition from English mores to
those of Italy; each novel concentrates upon the animal sexuality of
the Italian male. Forster's Gino is seen always in terms of furtive
animal movement, and the campanile of Airolo fittingly presides
over an atmosphere charged with sexuality. Lawrence's Cicio seems
always in physical movement, whether as part of the Natcha-kee-
tawara troupe, or on his ever-present bicycle. Lawrence, one notices,
has unaccountably dispensed with the campanile.

The ghost of Hardy's Sue hovers over these two novels. Madame
Kishwegin, in *The Lost Girl*, exclaims to Alvina: "But your Sue now,
in Jude the Obscure [*sic*] – is it not an interesting book?" (150).
Madame's remark signals the fact that Alvina Houghton and Lilia
Herriton, like Sue, are studies in repression, characters tortured by
an ambivalence of fear and need. Indeed, a comparison of these three
characters – Sue, Lilia, Alvina – offers an illuminating illustration of
the changing treatment of the theme of sexual repression from
Hardy through Lawrence. Sue remains always tortured and devoid
of self-knowledge. Not only is she destroyed; she destroys others.
Forster's Lilia is destroyed too, but she dies, as it were, from the
strenuous effort she has made to break the bonds of conventionality.
In Lawrence's novel, Alvina survives, and the reader knows she is re-
born. Hardy's tone is bitter; Forster's is sad and subdued, but quietly
hopeful; Lawrence's is vibrant and optimistic.

Hardy's use of the symbolism of music becomes, in Forster, a vital
and constant technique. Gino sings frequently, with gusto and a full
throat; but "herein he differed from Englishmen, who always have a
little feeling against music, and sing only from the throat, apologetic-
ally" (*Where Angels*, 127). Forster's Schlegel sisters meet Leonard

Bast at a London concert, and at the beginning they "only connect" through their discussions of music (*Howards End*, 42–53). Lawrence's Cicio is, of course, a guitarist–singer, whose threnodic serenade outside Alvina's window (*Lost Girl*, 288), as she symbolically delivers another woman's child, prepares the way for her own surrender to Cicio.

In these novels, Forster and Lawrence are developing themes which were introduced by Thomas Hardy. Thus when Lawrence feels the need to redefine for himself the nature and purpose of the novel as a literary form, he does so in terms of an examination of the fiction of Thomas Hardy. When Lawrence writes about the novels of Hardy, he is providing the central critical apology for the naturist movement – a movement which began with Hardy, and of which Lawrence is himself the culmination.

5 Hardy and Lawrence

"What a miserable world," wrote Lawrence to the literary agent J. B. Pinker in September 1914. "What colossal idiocy, this war. Out of sheer rage I've begun my book about Thomas Hardy. It will be about anything but Thomas Hardy, I am afraid – queer stuff – but not bad."[1] Most critics take Lawrence at his own word and find that the essay has little or nothing to do with Hardy. In this they are mistaken. Lawrence's view of Hardy may be partial, but his insights are true to the spirit of Hardy – when, that is, Lawrence chooses to talk of Hardy's novels themselves. Large portions of the "Study of Thomas Hardy," however, are devoted to a working out of Lawrence's own metaphysics of sexuality, and this is a subject which can and does take him far afield. In these sections Lawrence is providing, as he puts it, "a sort of Story of My Heart, or a Confessio Fidei."[2] Yet both Lawrence's criticism of the Hardy novels and his own far-ranging speculations are germane to our inquiry. Lawrence's study of Hardy, his longest critical work, is the most important expository document of the naturist movement, for several reasons. It serves clearly to set apart and underline those characteristics of Hardy which most appealed to Lawrence and his colleagues; it indicates the reasons why Lawrence borrows wholesale or modifies certain of Hardy's techniques for use in his own novels; and finally, it furnishes a partial but illuminating study of the transition from the Victorian to the twentieth-century novel. Lawrence's reading of Hardy serves to render explicit many of the themes which had remained muted in Hardy, but which had taken on a new urgency during the Edwardian period.

This essay on Hardy is also an implicit admission by Lawrence of his debt as a novelist to Hardy. The debt was large, especially in the novels of Lawrence's early period (1908–13). Between his first novel, *The White Peacock* (begun in 1906 and published in 1911), and his third, *Sons and Lovers* (1913), Lawrence is seeking his own voice and style; and if he eventually moves away from Hardy to create a new kind of novel, his point of origin is the ground which Hardy had prepared. That ground is the landscape of Wessex, and the unhappy humans moving across it.

Landscape occupies the center of Lawrence's attention throughout his study of Hardy. At first glance, this assertion might seem untrue, for a large part of the study is given over to a discussion of Lawrence's theory of male–female polarity. If the essay begins with the Hardy-like image of man's "struggle to feel at home on the face of the earth,"[3] it ends when "the two clasp hands, a moment, male and female . . . when the two fling their arms about each other . . . and when they kiss, on the mouth . . ." (516). The reader is entitled to wonder what all this love-making has to do with a tranquil Wessex landscape. Yet this relationship between setting and character, between spirit of place and sexual love, is the key, not only to Lawrence's essay, but also to his special quality as a novelist.

What Lawrence appreciates above all in Hardy is "his feeling, his sensuous understanding" (480). For Lawrence, Hardy's "understanding" is embodied in his landscape, not in his characters: "Putting aside his metaphysic, which must always obtrude when he thinks of people, and turning to the earth, to landscape, then he is true to himself" (480). Years later Aldous Huxley will say much the same kind of thing about Lawrence. "A walk in the country," Huxley writes, "was a walk through that marvelously rich and significant landscape which is at once the background and the principal personage of his novels."[4] Lawrence similarly sees Egdon Heath as a "principal personage"; for only Egdon has a prevailing purpose: "Not Egdon is futile. . . . What is futile is the purpose of man" (415).

What meaning does Hardy's landscape, as a "principal personage," hold for Lawrence? He sees Egdon and the Wessex landscape as possessing a moral authority which transcends any human activity: "This is a constant revelation in Hardy's novels: that there exists a great background, vital and vivid, which matters more than the people who move upon it" (419). We are reminded of Doughty's Arabia, Butler's Alps, Darwin's Patagonia, where landscape brought man back to himself, to his true nature. For these writers landscape was an instrument of man's salvation; but Lawrence is stating the proposition in a new way. Landscape is now an end in itself, independent of the motives of man. For Lawrence, Hardy's "people move in his landscape almost insignificantly somewhat like tame animals wandering in the wild" (480).

The words "tame" and "wild" provide a key to the imagery of Lawrence's early novels. We recall Mrs. Yeobright's journey through "independent worlds of ephemerons . . . passing their time in mad carousal . . . heaving and wallowing with enjoyment." Thus Lawrence describes the woods off the vale of Nethermere, in his first novel:

> The hyacinths drooped magnificently with an over-weight of purple, or they stood pale and erect, like unripe ears of purple corn. Heavy bees swung down in a blunder of extravagance among the purple flowers. They were intoxicated with the sight of so much blue. The sound of their hearty, wanton humming came clear upon the solemn boom of the wind overhead. The sight of their clinging, clambering riot gave satisfaction to the soul. (213)

Lawrence's operative words – "blunder," "extravagance," "intoxicated," "wanton," "riot" – are synonyms for Hardy's. The luxuriant, orgiastic build of Lawrence's paragraph is a duplication of Hardy's. Lawrence's repetition of gerunds – "humming," "clinging," "clambering" – echo Hardy's "passing," "heaving," "wallowing."

The best writing in *The White Peacock* – and parts of the novel are very good – is landscape description in direct imitation of the Hardy of *Return* or *Woodlanders*. Most of the pages of Lawrence's first novel evoke the same "leafy, sappy passion and sentiment of the woodlands" ("Study," 419), which he saw as Hardy's special world. Like Hardy's novels, *Peacock* is topographically "mapped" with painstaking attention. Lawrence utilizes the set tableaux, the purple passages, the word-painting of Hardy's early work; he pauses periodically, like Hardy, to evoke such rhythms of nature as the passing of one season to the next. Lawrence is still beholden to the Victorian method of scene construction: from setting to action to dialogue. He is particularly fond of several of Hardy's devices which have become clichés by 1911: the inevitable country fair, which Lawrence uses twice in *Peacock*; the local-color dialect characters such as the deaf old Mrs. Mays or the gruff old gamekeeper Annable, both close to the soil and the wisdom of folklore. The handy novelistic device of dipsomania, which Hardy employed clumsily but sparingly in *Jude*, Lawrence appropriates with a vengeance in the portraits of Frank Beardsall, at the beginning of the novel, and of George Saxton, at the end. George's drunkenness, it might be added, is expressed in an image of landscape: "A Prospect Among the Marshes of Lethe."

The chief symbols in *Peacock* are again borrowings from Hardy. Throughout the work, animals – a cat, a hedgehog, innumerable rabbits – are being caught and mangled in traps. This symbolism relates to the eventual entrapment of George Saxton in marriage, a theme which continues through Lawrence's work. Lawrence's imagery recalls the scarecrow incident, the slaughtered pig, and the trapped rabbit in *Jude the Obscure*. George Saxton's entrapment, like Jude's, is part of a larger historical theme: the decline of the rural yeoman. Cyril, the narrator of the novel, returns to the vale of Nethermere in his later years as a citified stranger; George, the erstwhile robust farmer, has left the land to become first a socialist soap-box orator, then a horse dealer and a drunkard.

Finally Lawrence derives his character configuration in *Peacock* from Hardy's *Jude the Obscure*. Lawrence's Lettie repeats Sue Bridehead's pattern of behavior: both fear physical sex; both are placed between two men of opposing characteristics. Cyril is a pale version of Paul Morel; Emily, though undeveloped as a character, is clearly a prototype of Miriam – sensitive, but inhibited and "mental," and thus another reflection of the Sue who is the model for a long line of Lawrentian heroines.

The White Peacock, then, reflects the spirit of Hardy on every level of theme and technique. Above all, Lawrence has invested his landscape with those elements of teeming fertility, wild abandon, and secret wisdom which were the hallmarks of Hardy's nature description. Thus when Lawrence boasts to Jessie Chambers about the initial critical reaction to *Peacock*, it is clear that he accepts a comparison with Hardy as the highest form of praise. "He told us," Jessie Chambers writes, "knowing how we should appreciate the valuation, that some of the descriptions of nature were considered equal to those in Hardy's *Tess of the d'Urbervilles*."[5]

Lawrence is still unsure, in his first novel, how to relate his characters to his landscape. Nature description may reflect and heighten Cyril's moods, but landscape here remains an extension of human emotion, rather than an independent source of mood and event. The trapped animals, for example, appear always at a distance which is emphasized by the reporting voice of Cyril. Never do we see a character reacting directly and dramatically to these trap-incidents, as Gerald and Gudrun will react to the caged, clawing rabbit in *Women in Love*,[6] or as Paul will react to Miriam's crushed flower in *Sons and Lovers*.[7] Lawrence's humans still move, as Hardy's do, in a world ultimately set apart from the processes of nature. The two worlds are connected, in *Peacock*, by means of the sensitive vision of Cyril, the first-person narrator. Yet both the landscape description and the character configuration of *Peacock* adumbrate Lawrence's later technique. Lawrence devotes twenty-two pages of analysis to Hardy's last novel in his study of Hardy, and his critique leaves little doubt that the dialectical arrangement of characters toward which Lawrence is moving, and which he first realizes effectively in *Sons and Lovers*, has its source in Hardy's *Jude the Obscure*.

Hardy's last novel is prefaced by a misogynistic outburst from Esdras:

> Yea, many there be that have run out of their wits for women, and become servants for their sakes. Many also have perished, have erred, and sinned, for women. . . . O ye men, how can it be but women should be strong, seeing they do thus?

These words would fit equally well as an inscription for *Sons and Lovers*. Strong women – Sue, Arabella, Miriam, Mrs. Morel – dominate both novels, and both Jude Fawley and Paul Morel, in one way or another, "run out of their wits for women." Each novel centers upon the relationship between man and woman; in each novel one can find the same cluster of themes, all converging on this relationship: the new status of women; the institutions of marriage and the family; the problems of marital incompatibility, of disillusionment in love, and finally, of sexual inhibition. Both novels present a critique of orthodox Christianity, of academic education, of modern industrialism, of art and the problems of the artist. Both stories evolve from the same oppositions: town against country, man-made against natural things, commerce against art, spiritual against physical love. Both stories develop a symbolic counterpointing of architectural styles (Gothic, Norman, domestic, industrial); both are *Bildungsromane* portraying young artist-heroes who seek an education, yet find satisfaction only through working with their hands (Jude, stone-carving; Paul, sketching).

Lawrence notes approvingly that Hardy always writes "about becoming complete, or about the failure to become complete" (410). *Jude the Obscure* begins with the departure of Jude's beloved schoolmaster, Phillotson, and Jude's first purpose is to follow after him, along "the Ickneild Street and original Roman road" (17), to "the city of light," the "castle, manned by scholarship and religion" (25). Both scholarship and religion (and Phillotson too) will betray Jude: he will never become a schoolmaster. Paul Morel, on the other hand, does become one; but he is no less betrayed.

Both Jude and Paul seem trapped, dreaming of escape: Jude longs for Christminster (Oxford), repository of ancient wisdom, where language is the key to the gate of freedom. But he will find the gate locked against his entrance. Paul, conversely, seems finally to escape, through his mother's death, from the confinement of Nottinghamshire; yet the tight little industrial town, the suffocating interior of the working-class dwelling, are images which dominate *Sons and Lovers*. These "tight little houses" will remain a favorite Lawrentian image, for his characters' continual pilgrimage, like his own, seem less a search for Rananim than an escape from the psychic smoke and soot of industrial England. Jude's tortured cry at the opening of Hardy's novel ("How ugly it is here!" 10) will be taken up by Paul Morel, and indeed by all Lawrence's central characters. Jude will seek the sanctuary of the Gothic; Paul will find Wordsworthian refuge in the loneliness of landscape.

If Jude and Paul are "struggling to become complete," it is because neither is able in modern society to locate that area of experience where heart and mind, body and soul, can meet. Lawrence's "Study" is a continual meditation on Hardy's attempt to locate the roots of the affective life of his characters. Continuing this search, Lawrence inherits Hardy's despair over the mechanical deadness of modern institutions. For both novelists, modern intellectual life is sterile because it is cut off from its affective roots; and modern affective life is neurotic because it is smothered by cruelly arbitrary social conventions and institutions. This "dissociation of sensibility" – for T. S. Eliot, following Alfred North Whitehead, will restate the problem for the post-war world – is symbolized, in *Jude the Obscure*, by the relationship between the hero and two female characters. Hardy conceives Jude's struggle in terms of a group of oppositions: between the intellectual and the sensual, the social and the personal, the male and the female; between love and convention; between art and technology; between the mind and the hands. This pattern of antitheses evokes those presiding spirits of the late nineteenth century, Hegel and Darwin. But Hardy is far from exemplifying Hegel: he is writing Hegel's epitaph. Dialectic, along with natural selection, will be buried with Father Time. In this respect, *Jude the Obscure* belongs with "The Darkling Thrush": together, they effectively usher out the nineteenth century.

To accommodate this series of oppositions, Hardy constructs his plot action around a triangular character-plan: Sue and Arabella at the bases, Jude at the apex. A subordinate triangle is formed by Phillotson's relationship with both Sue and Jude. Lawrence follows a closely identical plan in *Sons and Lovers*. When he began *Peacock*, Lawrence had envisaged a quadrangular arrangement involving two couples. "The usual plan," he remarked to Jessie Chambers, "is to take two couples and develop their relationships. Most of George Eliot's are on that plan. Anyhow, I don't want a plot, I should be bored with it. I shall take two couples for a start" (*Record*, 103).

There is nothing remarkable in this arrangement, taken in the light of nineteenth-century plot conventions. But the form it was actually to assume, in both *Peacock* and *Sons*, owes a good deal less to George Eliot than to Thomas Hardy. Both Hardy and Lawrence reduce the second male character (Phillotson in *Jude*, Leslie in *Peacock*, Dawes in *Sons*) to a peripheral and relatively static role.

If Lawrence did not want a plot, he succeeded admirably, by nineteenth-century standards. Where Hardy's novel is tightly structured around external plot-events, Lawrence's moves loosely from one subjective awareness to another. Thus in *Sons* there are two sets of character arrangements, one following the other chronologically, and each reflecting the same triangular pattern. During the first episodes, Paul is placed between Gertrude Morel and Miriam. Here Walter Morel is the secondary male character, standing between Gertrude and Paul. In the later episodes, Clara replaces Miriam, Gertrude remains as always the mother and rival-lover, with Baxter Dawes as the peripheral male, relating emotionally both to Clara and to Paul. Lawrence's remarks about Jude, in his "Study," suggest his debt to Hardy in this connection:

> Jude is only Tess turned round about. Instead of the heroine containing the two principles, male and female, at strife within her one being, it is Jude who contains them both, whilst the two women with him take the place of the two men to Tess. Arabella is Alec d'Urberville, Sue is Angel Clare. These represent the same pair of principles. (488)

Lawrence is here thinking of a combination of male–female "principles," and a consequent struggle between them, within a single character.

In both novels the note of sexual vitality and spontaneity is attached to one of the female characters: in *Jude*, Arabella; in *Sons*, Clara. Arabella is presented to the reader as "a complete and substantial female human – no more, no less" (42). When she hurls at Jude, with deadly aim, "a piece of flesh, the characteristic part of a barrow-pig" (41), we have her violence, her vulgarity, her sensu-

ality, not to speak of her somewhat heavy-handed humor. Hardy's
contrivance is sudden, surprising, crude, and in its crudeness lies it
effect. This blend of the repulsive and the attractive is characteristic
of Hardy's treatment of the sexual theme in *Jude*.

Like Arabella, Clara, in *Sons*, represents the sensual female un-
burdened by an oppressive spirituality. Lawrence draws Clara in
images of fleshly heaviness: swelling breasts, large hands, heavy arms.
Hardy's Arabella, though buxom, is a flat character, sketched from a
distance and with a boldness that approaches caricature; but
Lawrence's Clara is carefully rounded, finely shaded, and drawn with
a visual intensity that enlists the reader's empathy. The difference
is crucial: we have moved from Victoria to Edward VII. Jude never
achieves happiness with Arabella, but remains incomplete and torn
by his love for Sue: the flesh and the spirit never come together for
Jude. But Paul, moving away from Miriam to Clara, moves toward
that completeness Lawrence will record, however briefly, in *Women
in Love* and *Lady Chatterley's Lover*. Clara represents a kind of consummation that will be achieved fully, the reader senses, only after
the death of Gertrude Morel.

None of Lawrence's female characters changes radically during the
course of *Sons and Lovers*: each functions solely in her effect upon
Paul. Hardy's Sue Bridehead, on the contrary, is a complex and
changing character. Sue and Jude begin the novel at opposite poles;
at the end of the novel they are again at opposite poles, but they
have changed places. Sue begins as a pagan, Jude as a compliant
Christian. Jude is first presented wholly in spiritual terms, free of
fleshly preoccupations: bird-like innocence, naive reverence, great
expectations. Sue first appears to Jude in an ambience of sensuality,
freedom, vitality. But step by step, Sue becomes the symbol of law
over life, convention over freedom, pretentious morality over the
demands of the flesh; while Jude has moved through disenchantment
to rebellion and finally to despair. Yet if he has been lacerated and
destroyed by life, it is because he has sought no refuge.

Jude and Sue move simultaneously in opposite directions, on
parallel lines. The novel is dominated by the figure of parallels never
meeting, a characteristic Hardy symbol involving fatality and irony.
The novel is built structurally around this figure, which provides a
graphic emblem of the movement of both plot and character. At
their first meeting, Arabella and Jude walk in parallel lines on either
side of a stream (43); when Jude and Sue meet at the Cross of the
Martyrs, they "walk on in parallel lines" (117). The novel weaves

an intricate pattern of parallel locations, parallel marriages (Jude–Arabella, Sue–Phillotson), parallel lives (Jude–Father Time).

Sue represents, at the end of the novel, the tyranny of the spirit over the flesh; yet in the final analysis, the character of Sue cannot be embraced by any series of conventional attributes, and herein lies her importance as a character who represents a turning point in the English novel. Hardy uses the word "epicene" to describe Sue (84), yet it is doubtful whether he recognized that he had turned up – or perhaps stumbled upon – a new kind of material for English fiction. The combination of male and female in Sue (and Jude as well) forms the basis for a pattern of unresolved contradictions, and these contradictions are the key to Sue as a character. Her pattern of behaviour is repeated throughout the novel: she teases Jude verbally; when he responds as man to woman, she rejects him; then she feels remorse, and a deep need to be punished for her behaviour; she becomes expert at finding ways to punish herself. Her relationship with Phillotson echoes her dealings with Jude. At times, in fact, she teases the two simultaneously. Her lack of self-understanding, her total blindness to the pattern of her behaviour, means that she is condemned to repeat her mistakes, her "colossal inconsistencies." "You mustn't love me," she says to Jude. "You are to like me – that's all!" But a few days later she writes: "If you want to love me, Jude, you may" (186).

In Sue Bridehead Hardy created the first "modern" woman in English fiction. He is studying the destructive relationship between Sue's conscious life and the hidden, terrible forces of her unconscious. Hardy is pre-Freudian only in the sense that he lacks the vocabulary and the symbolism which, a generation later, will be part of the novelist's equipment. It is perhaps for this reason that Sue provides a pattern for Lawrence, who will treat this same subject matter throughout his writing career. Indeed Lawrence's analysis of Sue in his "Study of Thomas Hardy" reads precisely like his descriptions of Miriam in *Sons and Lovers*: Sue "wanted to live partially, in the consciousness in the mind only. . . . She was born with the vital female atrophied in her; she was almost male" (496). Sue Bridehead is the direct antecedent, not only of Lawrence's Miriam and Mrs. Morel, but also of Gudrun, Hermione, Mrs. Frank, and the countless neurotic women of his later fiction. Strong, masculine, spiritualized, "mental" women will dominate Lawrence's stories to the end. But with the intervention of Freud, Hardy's tragic contradiction will become Lawrence's psychological ambivalence.

If Hardy's plot involves opposing movement along parallel lines, Lawrence's Paul moves in a single (if crooked) line, from bondage to Miriam and Gertrude toward a liberation in his love for Clara. For it is precisely Miriam's likeness to his mother that makes it impossible for Mrs. Morel to like her. Jessie Chambers's remark that "Lawrence handed his mother the laurels of victory" (*Record*, 202) is hardly justified when Lawrence's work is seen as a whole: Gertrude Morel is the prototype, not of Lady Chatterley, but of the possessive women Lawrence so scorned.

Just as the narrative action of *Jude the Obscure* emerges from the attitudes and decisions of Sue, so Gertrude Morel dominates *Sons and Lovers*. Hardy leaves no doubt that Sue's masculine tendency to dominate is closely related to her sexual inhibitions. Lawrence, in turn, carefully traces Gertrude Morel's growing sexual disgust for her husband. As Sue is to the rustic Jude, so Gertrude is to the uncouth miner Walter Morel. If Sue jumps out of her bedroom window to avoid intercourse with Phillotson (277), Gertrude Morel provokes her detested husband to lock her out of the house (23). She turns from her husband first to William, and then to Paul, whose total allegiance she demands with the subtle masculine authority of a frustrated mother.

Paul seems unaware of his mother's possessiveness, just as Jude is unable to bring himself to recognize the depths of Sue's unconscious cruelty. It is Miriam who brings about Paul's first recognition. Like Sue, Miriam is first presented as sweet, guileless, feminine; but her willfulness soon appears, culminating in the scene where she fondles the daffodils, "sipping the flowers with fervid kisses." Paul accuses her of "clutching them as if you wanted to pull the heart out of them" (218). Like Sue, Miriam wants "mental" love; like Sue, she seems supremely oblivious of her inhibitions.

The epicene role of Hardy's Sue, then, is shared in *Sons* by Miriam and Mrs. Morel. The division suggests that Lawrence is more concerned than Hardy with the causes of the war between the sexes. Where Hardy resorts to a "family curse" cliché to explain Jude's bad marriage, Lawrence takes us back a generation to show the psychological effect of parent on child; in *The Rainbow* he traces through three generations the death of love. Where Hardy accepts the fact, placing the cause mysteriously outside character, Lawrence seeks a cause within the character.

Yet Hardy in his stark portrait of Father Time gives us within a few pages a rudimentary sketch of parental influence that will be

D

expanded and elaborated by Lawrence into his longest novel, *The Rainbow*. Father Time's total lack of contact with concrete physical being is a character-symbol of Lawrence's case against the deadly mental abstraction – scientific, religious, philosophical, and commercial – which he felt had become a substitute, in the modern world, for engagement in physical life itself. If this theme reaches its fullest expression in *The Rainbow* and *Women in Love*, it also pervades *Sons and Lovers*: when Paul fights against the abstract possessiveness in Miriam, he is objectifying an inner struggle. This *bellum intestinum* is the central preoccupation of the naturist movement; if it reaches a final statement in Lawrence, it had its beginning in Hardy.

Thus it comes as no surprise that Lawrence's first mention of his "book on Hardy" comes immediately after the completion of the last draft of *Sons and Lovers*.[8] The "Study" is built upon the proposition that "the effort to mate spirit with body, body with spirit, is the crying confusion and pain of our times" (474). Lawrence ranges widely from Renaissance painting to nineteenth-century poetry in order to illustrate the triumph of "law" over "love" in the modern world. "Law" is the conscious, mental, systematizing principle; "love" is the subconscious, instinctual, physical principle. " 'There is no reconciliation between Love and the Law,' says Hardy. 'The spirit of Love must always succumb before the blind, stupid, but overwhelming power of the Law' " (480). The terms of this opposition, it might be noted, are not Hardy's, but Lawrence's; and the notion that Hardy saw no possible "reconciliation" between the two principles is questionable. Yet Lawrence's insight into the struggle, in Hardy's novels, between individual spontaneity and social custom, is valid. Hardy's Father Time is a symbol of the death of physical sensibility in both Jude and Sue.

Lawrence's distinction between "law" and "love" recalls Hudson's "two laws" in *Green Mansions*: "For in that wood there is one law, the law that Rima imposes, and outside of it a different law" (119). Rima's law is the rule of nature: simple, spontaneous, instinctual. It is the law of the "green mansions," the landscape itself. The law is Rima's only in so far as she is an incarnation of the organic world; and her message is atavistic and incommunicable in language. Rima's law is not unlike that "primal morality greater than ever the human mind can grasp," which Lawrence sensed in Hardy's landscape ("Study," 419).

Like Hudson, Lawrence centers his attention upon the sub-human, physical world: "But somehow — that which is physic — non-human, in humanity, is more interesting to me than the old-fashioned human element. . . ."[9] Lawrence, like Hudson and Hardy, seeks always to suggest this "physic" life, this "non-human in humanity," in terms of landscape and nature description: ". . . there is a definite vibratory rapport between a man and his surroundings. . . ."[10] But in the "Study of Thomas Hardy" Lawrence suggests that landscape is not the only source of unknown, primal vitality. Man finds in woman those same qualities the earlier naturists had sought in "place": "She is the unknown, the undiscovered, into which I plunge to discovery, losing myself" (490). The word "she" has here supplanted the place-name we have come to expect: Egdon, Orinoco, Nepenthe, Nethermere. Lawrence has begun a process of identification between landscape and *eros* which will be summarized by Birkin, in *Women in Love*: "It isn't really a locality, though. It's a perfected relation between you and me . . ." (308).

6 Lawrence: A Version of Pastoral

T. E. Lawrence, whose extraordinary adventures resulted in large measure from his early infatuation with the Arabian landscape, published in 1927 a review of the novels of D. H. Lawrence. He wrote: ". . . and when the landscape painter in him feels the setting of a story, miracles happen."[1] Lawrence of Arabia had found the key to the originality of D. H. Lawrence's early novels: his use of landscape. Any account of Lawrence's development as a novelist between *Sons and Lovers* and *Women in Love* must center upon his attempts to find techniques of internalizing landscape – that is, of developing an idiom through which the subtle ebb and flow of the unconscious life of his characters might be charted through the device of nature description.

During these same years (1913–16), two new movements in poetry emerged, the Georgians and the Imagists. Lawrence was among the poets included in the *Georgian Poetry* anthologies of Edward March (1912–22). The Georgians resemble the naturists in their devotion to Thomas Hardy and to English rural life, but the two movements differ widely in respect to sensibility and technique. The Georgian poets represent perhaps the last murmur of nineteenth-century Romanticism, and as such lack the originality and the freshness of the naturist writers. Georgian prosody is unoriginal and tends toward sing-song; the emotions are stereotyped, the language vague and dream-like. Lawrence's poetry is closer, both in technique and in spirit, to the Imagists than to the Georgians. Like the Imagists, Lawrence seeks a new language of the emotions; objects to the use of metaphor as ornament; tries to objectify the whole sensibility including the unconscious; abhors abstractions; prefers shorter poetic forms.

Yet Lawrence is clearly no Imagist: he is moving, during these years, consciously and deliberately away from the idea of literature – poetry or fiction – as "picture-making." At the very time when Ezra Pound could reject the language of philosophy, as a poet, because

"It MAKES NO PICTURE,"[2] Lawrence is asserting that "the picture is really the death, and certainly the neurosis, of us all" (*Phoenix*, 381). Lawrence is looking in fact to that "pig-headed father" of Ezra Pound, Walt Whitman, whose poetic method depends less upon clearly visualized images than upon an eroticism of touch and upon slowly building, rolling rhythms of the ocean, rhythms which Whitman achieves largely through oratorical devices such as repetition, enumeration, invocation, and peroration. Lawrence was turning from pictures to music; and this new approach, which seems to have taken form during the writing of the "Study of Thomas Hardy," is the crucial factor in Lawrence's attempt to "internalize" the naturist landscape.

In February 1913 Lawrence had completed one hundred pages of the first version of a novel which was to appear eventually as *The Rainbow*. The new novel, he wrote to Garnett, "is all analytical – quite unlike *Sons and Lovers*, not a bit visualized."[3] This was a radical change, for graphic representation had played a primary role in Lawrence's early novels. In *Peacock*, aside from the sharply visual descriptions of Nethermere, Lawrence seemed to delight in bringing his lovers together over picture books. " 'Do you like pictures?' " Lettie asks George, and they contemplate "a pile of great books," and discuss Copley and Clausen interminably (25–7). Again, Cyril excitedly shows Emily some reproductions by Aubrey Beardsley; and when George sees the prints, they have an unmistakably erotic effect upon him: "And the more I look at these naked lines, the more I want her. It's a sort of fine sharp feeling, like these curved lines. I don't know what I'm saying – but do you think she'd have me? Has she seen these pictures?" (158–9). Lawrence's avid reading of Ruskin at the time seems to be reflected in the pages of his first novel. Paul Morel, like Lawrence himself, is a landscape artist, and the quality of description in *Sons and Lovers* reflects Paul's acute visual sensitivity.

Yet both early novels contain hints of the reasons for Lawrence's change in point of view. Paul, in *Sons*, is suspicious of "shapes": "The shape is a dead crust. The shimmer is inside really" (152). When Lettie, in *Peacock*, playfully casts herself as a Blessed Damozel, the earth-bound George Saxton replies – and in his reply we can detect the voice of the young novelist: "Hang thin souls, Lettie! I'm not one of your souly sort. I can't stand Pre-Raphaelites" (85). George's thesis is elaborated by Lawrence in his study of Hardy where, in a twenty-page digression, a capsule history of art from

Giotto through Botticelli to Turner exemplifies that "spiritualization" of modern culture to which Lawrence so strenuously objected. In later years Lawrence would find in the art of the Etruscans and of the Egyptians a graphic mode of representation still uncorrupted by modern self-consciousness.

For it was the "mental consciousness" of visual representation to which Lawrence objected: "Living as we do in the light of the mental consciousness, we think everything is as we see it and as we think it. Which is a vast illusion" (*Phoenix*, 635). Galileo, Lawrence suggested, has proved that we are not at the center of the universe, but we do not believe him: our eyes are egocentric; they lie. Lawrence believed that modern man is addicted to visual experience, and that his addiction is a symptom of his separation from physical life: "We see too much, we attend too much" (*Fantasia*, 102). A visual image presupposes a subject and an object separated by a physical distance, a relationship of opposition, not of unity: "A man very rarely has an image of a person with whom he is livingly, vitally connected. He has only dream-images of the persons who, in some way, *oppose* his life-flow and his soul's freedom, and so become impressed upon his plasm as objects of resistance" (*Fantasia*, 197).

Lawrence's insight was hardly original: the attempt to bridge the dualism between subject and object has been the constant pre-occupation of philosophers since Descartes. Even Karl Marx noted that "The chief defect in all hitherto existing materialism . . . is that the object, reality, sensuousness, is conceived only in the form of the *object* of contemplation but not as *human sensuous activity*. . . ."[4] And Samuel Butler's Overton, in *The Way of All Flesh*, concluded that

> in the end we shall be driven to admit the unity of the universe so completely as to be compelled to deny that there is either an external or an internal, but must see everything both as external and internal at one and the same time, subject and object – external and internal – being unified as much as everything else. This will knock our whole system over, but then every system has got to be knocked over by something. (265)

Butler, Hardy, and the travel-novelists sought to suggest this "unity of the universe" through visual description of place. Lawrence began, as a novelist, in this tradition; but increasingly he turned from the visual to the tactile and aural senses, from the static quality of graphic representation to the immediate and dynamic qualities of rhythm and touch.

Lawrence's thinking owed much to the Nietzschean distinction between the "Dionysian" and the "Apollonian" spirits. For Nietzsche, Apollo presides over the plastic arts, Dionysos over the musical; Apollo represents rationality and organization, Dionysos an atavistic orgy and intoxication. Apollo is post-Socratic, Dionysos primeval; Apollo analyses and divides into the oppositions of dramatic dialogue, Dionysos unifies into the intuitive rhythmic integrity of the tragic chorus. Thus Lawrence's preference for Egyptian over later Greek art, or for Etruscan over Italian painting, is analogous to Nietzsche's antipathy for Socrates and all his works. Both Nietzsche and Lawrence ultimately urged a balance between the two spirits; if they rhapsodized over the Dionysian qualities of experience it was because they felt modern man had become almost exclusively Apollonian. Lawrence was now striving to perfect those Dionysian descriptive techniques which had been present in Hardy's imagery of teeming organism, in Hudson's imagery of touch, odor, and musical sounds. Lawrence was confirming the naturists' distrust of logic and conceptual language, of static organization in both society and art. In short, he was carrying on the attempt of the naturists to discover a poetic correlative for the instinctual life of man.

Thus when Birkin and Ursula, in *Women in Love*, finally achieve that balance and equilibrium which was Lawrence's ultimate definition of love, Ursula yearns for the eyeless darkness, tactile immediacy, and sub-rational ecstasy represented by Nietzsche's Dionysos:

> She would have to touch him. To speak, to see, was nothing. It was a travesty to look and to comprehend the man there. Darkness and silence must fall perfectly on her, then she could know mystically, in unrevealed touch. She must lightly, mindlessly connect with him, have the knowledge which is the death of knowledge, the reality of surety in not knowing. (311)

Ursula's "mindless" connection may not be the only answer to Forster's inscriptive plea, in *Howards End*: "Only connect. . . ." Almost certainly it is not what Forster had in mind. Yet Lawrence's polarities, like Forster's, are preparations for bridge-building: the "arch" of *The Rainbow*, the "equilibrium" of *Women in Love*, the "duet" of *Aaron's Rod* are moments of connection, instants in which dualities are transcended or obliterated. Synthesis presupposes antithesis, and the novels of Lawrence's middle period are constructed around a complex, related series of oppositions.

Women in Love is the most striking (and the most successful) example of this process. The essentially triangular character-structure of the early novels, with the fourth character playing a minor role, becomes solidly quadrangular in *Women in Love*. The novel is built around counterpointing scenes between two pairs of lovers, Birkin–Ursula and Gerald–Gudrun. The themes are presented in a musical way: they are orchestrated by means of a constantly changing, kaleidoscopic interplay between four principles: male–female, "love"–"law." Each member of the love-quartet represents a different combination of these four components: Birkin and Ursula represent the male–female polarities of the liberating principle of "love"; Gerald and Gudrun of the confinement of "law."

The novel might well have been titled "Point Counter Point," for there is a deliberate and careful balancing and contrasting of scenes. For example, a chapter (xxiii) which describes the birth of love between Ursula and Birkin is followed by a chapter entitled "Death and Love," which reports both a physical death (Thomas Crich) and the extinction of love between Gerald and Gudrun; "Man to Man" (xvi), a scene between Gerald and Birkin, balances "Woman to Woman" (xxii), which involves the two sisters. This contrapuntal arrangement of both character pattern and story structure would seem on the surface too neat and schematic, but the contrasts are modulated and softened by means of a rich and varied play of antithetical symbols, each balanced by another. In regard to symbol, the governing duality of the novel is, as we might expect, an opposition of place: Lawrence is utilizing an established naturist convention. The opposition between "law" and "love," mind and matter, the spiritual and the animal, is represented by the pond of Willey Water, which is the center of action of the first part of the novel, and by the Swiss Alps, near Basel, where the quartet spend a skiing vacation. The lake is gained by descent, the Alps by ascent, aspiration; the lake suggests the female, the Alps the male; the lake is the womb of luxuriant plant life, the Alpine promontory is bare and lifeless, like Butler's; the lake is the locale of mindless organism, of Dionysos; the range of Alps is the home of idea, of consciousness, of Apollo.

Both locales, representing extremes as they do, are sources of death. Gerald's sister Diana dies by drowning in Willey Water, and her death is balanced by that of Gerald, who becomes confused and lost in the Alps and is frozen to death. The mountain peak, marked by "a half-buried crucifix, a little Christ under a little sloping hood" (465), is the home of the "mentalized" Gerald and Gudrun: ". . . the sledge drove away leaving Gudrun and Gerald standing in the snow, waving.

Something froze Birkin's heart, seeing them standing there in the isolation of the snow, growing smaller and more isolated" (431). The sledge, it might be noted, is carrying Ursula and Birkin on the first lap to Verona, home of Shakespeare's hot-headed young lovers.

Conversely, the lake is the refuge of Ursula and Birkin; but the Dionysian Birkin does not *see* the vegetation, he feels it, lying in the grass: "Nothing else would do, nothing else would satisfy, except this coolness and subtlety of vegetation travelling into one's blood" (100). The "mental" Gudrun, on the other hand, undergoes a "stupor of apprehension" at the sight of the suggestively turgid pond: "What she could see was mud, soft, oozy, watery mud, and from its festering chill, water-plants rose up, thick and cool and fleshy, very straight and turgid, thrusting out their leaves at right angles, and having dark lurid colours, dark green and blotches of black-purple and bronze" (111). Here Lawrence's landscape is not, like Hudson's, a "map of love"; it is an erotic emblem. Gudrun attempts to obliterate the obscenity of these images by the Baconian method of substituting botany for life: ". . . she *knew* how they rose out of the mud, she *knew* how they thrust out from themselves, how they stood stiff and succulent against the air" (111).

Gudrun's Baconian interest in causation is a recurring theme of *Women in Love*. The ghost of the Lord Chancellor lurks always behind the restless mentalizing of Hermione, Sir Joshua, Gudrun, and Gerald: "You are like Lord Bacon, Gerald," says Birkin (344); for Gerald, as a mine owner, "had a fight to fight with Matter, with the earth and the coal it enclosed. This was the sole idea, to turn upon the inanimate matter of the underground, and reduce it to his will. . . . Gerald was the God of the machine, Deus ex Machina" (220).

In the rarefied Baconian Alps of the mind and the will, Gudrun withers and Gerald dies. Yet the primitive lake of sensuality is equally hazardous. Birkin meditates upon an African carving of a woman and decides that in these Africans "the goodness, the holiness, the desire for creation and productive happiness must have lapsed, leaving the single impulse for knowledge in one sort . . . knowledge arrested and ending in the senses . . . knowledge such as the beetles have . . ." (245–6). Both the mud of Willey Water and the Alpine snows are, for humans, uninhabitable.

Lawrence's landscape in *Women in Love*, along with his description generally, is no longer a ground of all being. It is a series of signposts or points of reference in a shifting, mobile world of physical and psychological change. Lawrence's rejection of fixed visual imagery is part of his changing view of reality. For a writer's "definition" of human nature is intimately related to his quality of physical vision. During these years an ironic or tragic mood was inevitably embodied in a sharply visual style. One thinks, for example, of the unforgettable frieze of Tess dying among the pillars of Stonehenge as an image that attains a pathos by itself, independent of plot. Again, Conrad's evocative landscapes and seascapes, his bold use of chiaroscuro, or his firmly visualized bodily gestures and attitudes, are stylistic counterparts of his final irony. But Lawrence's purpose, from *The Rainbow* on, is precisely the opposite of Conrad's. In Lawrence the ironic tone is exceptional and subordinate, commenting always upon individuals rather than upon the human condition. Lawrence seeks, through a manipulation of prose rhythms and a pattern of sounds and textures, to evoke an impression of movement and change. Where Conrad's imagery suggests an immutable fixity beneath man's ephemeral hopes, Lawrence's avoidance of static imagery suggests that all is change, and that out of this change can come "a way to a better world."

Thus the challenge, for the lovers Birkin and Ursula, is to find a middle ground, a spirit of place in which this symphony of dualities can resolve into equilibrium. They find their homeland in a chapter which functions as the arch-stone of the novel. The chapter is called "Excurse" (xxiii), and tells the story of a ride in a motor car, a pilgrimage without apparent purpose or direction:

> "Where are we?" she asked suddenly.
> "Not far from Worksop."
> "And where are we going?"
> "Anywhere." (295)

For Birkin is tired of the serious business of "making connections," and has the impulse to "drift on in a series of accidents – like a picaresque novel." "Why not?" he wonders; "Why form any serious connections at all?" (293–4). Birkin's way of avoiding a "connection" with Ursula is to present her with several rings, to buy her affection. The rings in turn cause a bitter scene over Ursula's "spiritual" rival, Hermione. Birkin decides that between them there is little to choose: Hermione is "Idea," Ursula is "Womb," and "both were horrible" (301). Finally Ursula throws Birkin's sapphires in the mud; the fight ends, and they depart from "this memorable battlefield" (303).

After this inevitable Lawrentian battle of the sexes, Ursula and

Birkin stop at an inn where, in the yard, they hear the Southwell Minster bells playing a hymn. Ursula is transfixed; looking at Birkin, she "recalled again the old magic of the Book of Genesis, where the sons of God saw the daughters of men, that they were fair" (304). Diction and imagery here evoke memories of Eden; Ursula and Birkin forget the terrible knowledge of Eve after the Fall; and at last they are in love. But then the inevitable naturist question arises: " 'But where?' she said. 'I don't know,' he said." Birkin has faith that there is a locality, a place, for lovers: " 'There's somewhere where we can be free. . . .' 'But where?' she sighed." Now Birkin betrays the ultimate secret of the Lawrentian travel novel. "It isn't really a locality, though. It's a perfected relation between you and me, and others – the perfect relation – so that we are free together" (307–8).

The "perfect relation," the balance, has been achieved: Birkin has struck an equilibrium between the "lambent intelligence" of the Greek and the "pure Egyptian concentration in darkness" (310). And Ursula "hung in a pure rest, as a star is hung, balanced unthinkably." Her one desire is to empty her eyes, so that "with perfect fine finger-tips of reality she would touch the reality in him . . ." (311).

Ursula and Birkin have discovered their inner Eden, and have resumed their motor-car excursion. But as they pass among "great old trees," Ursula again remembers that a perfected relation must have a locality, a spirit of place, somewhere between Willey Water and the Alps; and once again she asks Birkin for their bearings: " 'Where are we?' she whispered. 'In Sherwood Forest.' It was evident he knew the place" (312). Birkin has at last located the modern English Eden: it is the forest home of the pastoral ballad hero-rebel, Robin Hood. And Birkin recognizes that they have found their locality, their resting place between the mud and the stars. As they drive among the oaks of the forest, they come to a place where "the green lane widened into a little circle of grass, where there was a small trickle of water at the bottom of a sloping bank." Birkin knows that this is the pastoral place of freedom, the setting of Genesis, the land of Rima and Mowgli and Kim, of Lilia and Alvina and Denis. Birkin stops the car. " 'We will stay here,' he said, 'and put out the lights.' "

In the darkness of Sherwood Forest, we recall that primal sightless beginning, in the Book of Genesis, when "the earth was without form, and void; and darkness was upon the face of the deep." From Egdon Heath at dusk to Sherwood Forest at night, this primeval darkness is a reminder that in the beginning was unity. Indeed the endings of Lawrence's novels – *Sons, Rainbow, Women, Aaron's Rod,*

The Fox – are always beginnings, as if Lawrence were trying to wind back through the labyrinthine sins of civilization to recapture the fresh hope of those first words of memory. "In the beginning."

The quest for Eden is a quest for unity. Beneath the profusion of polarities in *Women in Love* lies the integrity of the pastoral mood. For the spirit of pastoral is the spirit of comedy, of reconciliation; and the source of that spirit of unity in pastoral is neither man nor God, but physical nature. The goal of that spirit is well expressed in the biological image of Edgar, in *King Lear*: "Men must endure / Their going hence, even as their coming hither: / Ripeness is all." In the novels of Lawrence, the search for roots ends with an imagery of organic ripeness, in a mythic world of pastoral idyll.

E. M. W. Tillyard has suggested that "the myth of retirement" is one of the rare indigenous mythic conventions in an English culture which has borrowed its mythology largely from the ancient Greeks. Tillyard traces the myth from Horace and Virgil through Marvell's "The Garden" to *Robinson Crusoe* and Cowper's *The Task*; in modern times Tillyard suggests, "the classic example of the same process is D. H. Lawrence, whose life from one side could be called a series of attempts to find the right place to retire. . . ."[5] Lawrence's unending search for Rananim suggests that the myth was all too real for Lawrence the man. But for Lawrence the novelist, and for his fellow naturists as well, the myth was an expression of an ultimate view of the nature of man, and of man's relationship to the earth he inhabits. For Lawrence and the naturists were in full revolt against the myths of the Christian tradition, the "ordering" dualisms of God–man, heaven–hell, angel–animal, free will–predestination. These Christian polarities had combined, in the post-Reformation world, with an epistemological dualism which had set the mind of man inalterably apart from physical reality. Finally, with the industrial revolution had come that crowning separation which was represented by Henry Adams in the symbols of the dynamo and the Virgin, and by Lawrence in the images of the machine and the flower. It was the purpose of Hardy, Lawrence, and the naturists to break through these man-made dichotomies, to find a new language of unity, to forge a myth that would embody Forster's vague admonition: "Only connect. . . ."

In their attempt to make this "connection," the naturists were ironically constrained to utilize the very terms to which they objected: they were often caught speaking abstractly about the dangers of abstraction, generalizing about the futility of generalization, or being acutely conscious of the enervating effects of acute consciousness. To this criticism Lawrence would reply that "we must know, if only in order to learn not to know" (*Fantasia*, 112). Counteracting this undeniable dilemma was the strength of the naturist myth itself, embodying, often in clumsy and ill-organized tales of travel, a strong faith in the unifying, reconciling fact of physical organism. Eden is the place of genesis, of physical birth. Birkin, in "Excurse," is "like a thing that is born, like a bird when it comes out of an egg, into a new universe" (303). Eden is the place of childhood where Rabelais' "fays ce que vouldras" is the law. Birkin is like "an infant, that breathes innocently, beyond the touch of responsibility" (301).

This childhood release from moral imperatives, from Ibsen's "claims of the ideal," was expressed by the naturists in an imagery of play: the "great game" of *Kim*, the "hide-and-seek" of *Green Mansions*, the amoral "playground" of *South Wind*. Lawrence's heroes and heroines also move inevitably away from a situation of work toward a condition of play. Gerald, the mine owner, goes skiing in the Alps; Aaron, the coal miner, goes cavorting in Italy; Paul Morel resigns as clerk, Ursula resigns as schoolteacher; Kate retreats to Mexico, Constance Chatterley to a groom's cottage.

In his study of Hardy, Lawrence noted admiringly that none of Hardy's characters "care very much for money" (410); he applauded their instinct to live "wildly and with gorgeousness" (398); and his highest commendation for Hardy's people is that they are constantly doing "unreasonable things":

> They are always going off unexpectedly and doing something that nobody would do. . . . These people of Wessex are always bursting suddenly out of bud and taking a wild flight into flower, always shooting suddenly out of a tight convention. . . . Nowhere, except perhaps in Jude, is there the slightest development of personal action in the characters: it is all explosive. (410)

The word "explosive" might well be used to describe the plot structure of Lawrence's own novels, for they lack any suggestion of a chain of causal connection. The violent outburst experienced by Birkin and Ursula in "Excurse" occurs in a plot vacuum: an automobile trip with no destination, a "series of accidents – like a picaresque novel."

Lawrence's use of the word "explosive" also reminds us that, for all his apparent dislike of science, he was quick to exploit the language of the new technology. The spontaneous explosion was antithetical for Lawrence to the automatic machine. Again, Lawrence was one of the first English writers to employ the symbolism of electricity. The image of electric current provided a fitting non-visual expression of Lawrence's cherished theme of sexual polarity: "It was a dark flood of electric passion she released from him, drew into herself. She had established a rich new circuit, a new current of passional electric energy, between the two of them, released from the darkest poles of the body and established in perfect current" (*Women*, 305–6). The electric current, like the explosion, is an image of freedom: between the two poles, and because of them, the individual floats free, in equilibrium. Beneath the pattern of oppositions in *Women in Love* lies the unity of pastoral in an age of electricity.

The explosive, unmotivated, free act which Lawrence remarked in Hardy's characters, and which became a literary convention in the naturist novel, is a symbol of revolt. But where the traditional pastoral hero retires to the mythical simplicity of the sheepfold in revolt against the immorality and corruption of the city, the exploding action of Lawrence's pastoral hero is directed against both Christian idealism and scientific determinism. And his manner of exploding represents his attempt to avoid the language and the concepts of Christian morality. The explosive act, like Gide's gratuitous act, is beyond causality: it is the action of a man not as he orders or understands nature, but as he is the supreme expression *of* nature. It is the action of the pastoral swain whose identity with nature takes the form, not of words, but of song; whose "oaten pipe" speaks a language beyond words.

Lawrence's adaptation of pastoral elements began with his first novel. *The White Peacock* was written by a young school teacher and has all the clumsy literary allusions which are so tempting to the novelist freshly emerged from the academy. What might be called "parlor pastoral" is a game continually played by the characters in *Peacock*. Cresswell, a classics student, meditates upon George Saxton sharpening his scythe: "Lord, a giddy little pastoral – fit for old Theocritus, ain't it. . . . You say any giddy thing in a pastoral. . . . Who's that tuning his pipe? – oh, that fellow sharpening his scythe!" (226–7). Cresswell's "literary" pastorals were meant of course to be contrasted with Lawrence's "real" pastoral; it was not the pastoral theme, but the pastoral artifice, to which Lawrence objected, and his subsequent development as a novelist involved his attempt to recast themes of pastoral for the twentieth century.

The most sustained example of Lawrence's use of this pastoral convention occurs in *Aaron's Rod* (1922). It is one of Lawrence's most uneven and ill-organized works; yet it illustrates, perhaps more dramatically than any other of his books, both Lawrence's doctrine and his method as a practitioner of the pastoral travel novel. It also indicated the pervasiveness of Lawrence's debt to naturist conventions. For Hardy's Gabriel Oak and Hudson's Mr. Abel had provided a pattern for Lawrence's Aaron Sisson: the Old Testament shepherd, the pastoral nomad, the oaten pipes. But in *Aaron's Rod*, Lawrence gave a new expression to the myth of pastoral retirement, and a new meaning to its musical symbolism. It is a symbolism suggested by Lawrence's description of an Etruscan tomb-painting: "The Etruscan young woman . . . is quite serene, and dancing herself as a very fountain of motion and of life, the young man opposite her dancing himself the same, in contrast and balance, with just the double flute to whistle round their naked heels."[6]

The double flute is an apt image of the central theme of *Aaron's Rod*. For Aaron's rod is his flute, and his search, throughout the story, is to find another flute, another voice, to sing along with his, in freedom and equality, "in contrast and balance." For a brief moment, Aaron seems to find the other voice: he brings his flute to play for the Marchesa del Torre, "a modern Cleopatra brooding, Antony-less,"[7] and she in turn is to sing for him. She tries a French song, but her voice wavers: "It's no good," she says, "I can't sing." Aaron sounds the note on his flute for her to begin again, but she cannot:

> So he played the melody alone. At the end of the verse, he looked up at her again, and a half-mocking smile played in his eyes. Again he sounded the note, a challenge. And this time, as at his bidding, she began to sing. The flute instantly swung with a lovely soft firmness into the song, and she wavered only for a minute or two. Then her soul and her voice got free, and she sang. . . . For the first time her soul drew its own deep breath. (248)

As for Aaron, in this moment "he had got it back, the male godliness, the male godhead" (250). Aaron's flute symbolizes his individuality, his creativity, his manliness, his freedom. But perhaps most of all, his flute represents the inner vibration of his being, the voice of his blood: "He was a musician . . . his thoughts and his ideas, were dark and invisible, as electric vibrations are invisible no matter how many words they may purport" (160).

Aaron Sisson, then, is a man, not of words, but of vibrations, of music. Lawrence conceives his character largely in terms of images of sound, just as Hudson had done with Rima; and it is with this pattern of images that we are concerned.

The opening chapter of *Aaron's Rod* is dominated by the sound of the voice of Aaron's wife. She is never visualized; she, like the children, is not seen, but only heard, shouting. And when little Millicent, Aaron's daughter, half-intentionally smashes the blue ball, a Christmas decoration out of Aaron's past, the explosion rings out like a clash of cymbals in a squabbling cacophony of family voices. (This explosion will be repeated at the end of the book, for Aaron's flute is destroyed by a bomb.) A page later we hear the counter-theme, the sound of "music, soft and rich and fluid" (9). Aaron is playing his flute.

From the beginning Aaron has been presented largely in terms of his sensitivity to sounds: "As he sat he was physically aware of the sounds of the night: the bubbling of water in the boiler, the faint sound of the gas, the sudden crying of the baby in the next room, then noises outside, distant boys shouting, distant rags of carols, fragments of voices of men" (8). So Aaron plays, but the melody of his flute sounds as a lonely voice in a hostile environment: the reader is asked to believe that even his children hated the sound. "He was playing Mozart. The child's face went pale with anger at the sound" (10).

We next hear the sound of music at the opera in London, where Aaron has found employment after leaving his wife. Josephine Ford, Jim Bricknell, Lilly, and Struthers are sitting in a tight little box watching a shoddy performance of *Aida*. The sets are "sham Egypt" (42), the singers are fat and orange with Egyptian make-up. Josephine's face expresses a silent *"Merde!"* While the love story unfolds, the guests discuss love. The following chapter (iv, entitled "Talk") consists entirely of bloodless pseudo-sophisticated talk about love, all of it as false as the performance of *Aida*.

The symbolism of music is further developed in the episode describing Aaron's visit with Sir William and Lady Franks at Novara (xiii). Lady Franks, a deadly, possessive woman is, we learn, "afraid of music itself" (163), although she plays the piano. But Beethoven is at the service of Lady Franks's material possessiveness; he is merely an extension of her will: "Yes – he makes me feel the same faith: that what I lose will be returned to me. Just as I found my cloak" (165). Later Lady Franks plays the piano in another room, trying to draw Aaron from conversation with her husband: "And the ripple of the music contained in it the hard insistence of the little woman's will" (171). Lady Franks offers to accompany Aaron and his flute, but it is clear that Aaron wants to play alone.

Aaron's conversation with Lady Franks introduces a new musical idea which will be developed in later episodes with the Marchesa in Florence: the distinction between melody and harmony. Aaron favors the single, unaccompanied voice: "I wish we could go back to melody pure and simple." But the good lady stands firmly opposed:

> "Do you really. I shouldn't say so: oh no. But you can't mean that you would like all music to go back to melody pure and simple! Just a flute – just a pipe! Oh, Mr. Sisson, you are bigoted for your instrument. I just *live* in harmony – chords, chords!" She struck imaginary chords on the white damask, and her sapphires swam blue. (132)

Here the single unhampered voice of Aaron's flute is contrasted with the playing of chords which modify the individuality of the single voice and force harmonic "rules" upon it, just as Aaron's marriage had applied coercion to love. For "harmony" is precisely Aaron's problem: "harmonizing" in love or friendship, without becoming subject to the other person. Aaron had escaped the jarring "harmony" of marriage only to be caught in the powerful charisma of Lilly. Toward the end of the novel, with the Marchesa, Aaron states his problem plainly: "What I can't stand is chords, you know: harmonies" (221). And finally, Aaron brings the themes of love and music explicitly together: "I don't believe in harmony and people loving one another. I believe in the fight and nothing else. . . . I believe in the fight of love, even if it blinds me" (255–6).

And so the fight occurs: one melody, two voices, Aaron playing, the Marchesa singing, the female principle of harmony submitting totally to the male melody. For the Marchesa, Aaron's flute is "like a pure male voice – as a blackbird's when he calls" (246). But mating calls, for Lawrence, have a way of going off-pitch, and the blossoming of Aaron's rod is short lived. "So you blossom, do you? – and thorn as well," says Aaron (250). After two nights in the Marchesa's boudoir, Aaron feels the harmony closing in. Cleopatra is beginning to win, and Antony makes his escape. "Cleopatra," muses Aaron, "killed her lovers in the morning. Surely they knew that death was their just climax" (265).

And indeed the next chapter (xx) is about death in Florence. First we see three men kneeling over a mysterious object that turns out to be a corpse. But the important death is yet to come, the death of

Aaron's rod. For while Lilly is speaking of the "stinking" death of the ideal of love, "the beastly Lazarus of our idealism" (271), there occurs the culminating sound-effect of the novel: "CRASH! There intervened one awful minute of pure shock, when the soul was in darkness" (273). An anarchist's bomb, like God out of a machine, has shattered the calm of the outdoor café, and the music of Aaron's flute, which lies splintered. "Throw it in the river," Lilly says; "It's an end" (275).

After the explosion which destroys Aaron's rod, there is no more music. A few lines later begins a new, and last, chapter entitled "Words." "With the breaking of the flute, that which was slowly breaking had finally shattered at last. And there was nothing ahead: no plan, no prospect" (279). There are no more goals, but then "goals" are "gaols" as Lilly remarks, playing with "words" (282). For the treacherous sounds of human speech have replaced the vibrant pastoral melodies of Aaron's rod.

This novel is not one of Lawrence's best. It lacks unity of structure and coherence of theme. Indeed, it almost succeeds in not being a novel at all: it begins as a retirement tale, continues as a travel book, and lapses too often into a series of strident sermons. The novel is episodic, a kind of reverse *Odyssey*, a voyage away from Penelope's knitting domesticity, rather than homewards to Ithaca. But the act of running away, once performed, deprives this novel – like Butler's *Way* or Wells's *Polly* – of the specific goal that is needed to hold an *Odyssey* together.

Yet Lawrence's book provides a fitting climax to our account of the travel novel: it not only illustrates the decline of the naturist genre, it also brings us back to the source of naturism in Hardy. For Aaron's sustained effort to "connect," to make the voice of his flute part of a duet, inevitably recalls the moment, in *Far from the Madding Crowd*, when "suddenly an unexpected series of sounds began to be heard. . . . They were the notes of Farmer Oak's flute" (10). Gabriel Oak's flute is heard at night, "on the eve of St. Thomas's, the shortest day of the year," from the interior of a shepherd's hut among the flock; Aaron's is first heard on Christmas eve, and he is playing a "sixteenth-century Christmas melody" (9). Like Aaron, Gabriel dreams of making his flute part of a duet, with Bathsheba: "I can make you happy," Gabriel says to Bathsheba. "You shall have a piano in a year or two – farmers' wives are getting to have pianos now – and I'll practise up the flute right well to play with you in the evenings" (32). And Bathsheba replies, "Yes; I should like that," but her notion of marriage has the same Cleopatran ring as the Marchesa's ". . . a marriage would be very nice in one sense. People would talk about me and think I had won my battle, and I should feel triumphant, and all that. But a husband – " (33).

Farmer Oak knows it is useless to argue: like Aaron, he is a man of music, not of words: "Oak had nothing finished and ready to say as yet, and not being able to frame love phrases which end where they begin; passionate tales – Full of sound and fury – Signifying nothing – he said no words at all" (26). Thus Gabriel's duet, like Aaron's, comes only after many pages of solo sounds. Finally, after an evening of ballads rendered by Joseph Poorgrass, when Bathsheba Everdene is requested to sing " 'The Banks of Allan Water," she at last turns to Farmer Gabriel Oak: "Have you brought your flute?' she whispered. 'Yes, miss.' 'Play to my singing, then' " (178). Gabriel's flute "swelled to a steady clearness"; and the ensuing duet between Oak and Bathsheba is the prelude to their final matrimonial harmony.

Lawrence never admitted his "borrowing" from Hardy in *Aaron's Rod*, but then Lawrence never admitted borrowing anything from anybody. In the case of *Aaron's Rod* and *Far from the Madding Crowd*, the influence is perceptible not only in terms of the obvious "coincidence" of pastoral symbol, but also, and more importantly, in terms of the specific use of the flute as an emblem of the insufficiency of verbal communication. For the problem of communication, of forging a coherent symbolic language in an increasingly chaotic and fragmented world, is the paramount issue in the literature of the twentieth century. Yeats constructed an elaborate field-theory of myth; Joyce with equal industry erected a capacious mythic scaffolding to support the minor peregrinations of a bourgeois Jew on a Dublin day; Bernard Shaw borrowed from Darwin, Marx, Ibsen, and Butler to forge a new dramatic idiom; Proust, tasting a madeleine, found a principle of unity in the subjective associations and regurgitations of memory; Forster aspired to mindful connections, Lawrence descended to an organic unity of mindless vibrations.

Each of these writers was obsessed by a suspicion that people are no longer communicating, that rational discourse has been stripped of meaning and relevance. Each in his own way was attempting to express an insight which resists conceptualization: the intuition that human "relatedness," whether in personal love or in social fellowship, is rooted, not in conscious spiritual "meanings," but in unconscious physical organism. Each was asserting, with Montaigne, that "la peste de l'homme, c'est l'opinion de savoir" ("man's plague is that he thinks he knows"); with Marx and Engels that "it is not consciousness that determines life, but life that determines consciousness"; with Ezra Pound, "go in fear of abstractions"; with Yeats, "the abstract is not life and everywhere draws out its contradictions"; and with Lawrence's fervent American admirer, William Carlos Williams: "Say it, no ideas but in things."

7 Toward Freud

"Shakespeare," wrote E. M. Forster, "was subconsciously aware of the subconscious, so were Emily Brontë, Herman Melville and others. But conscious knowledge of it only comes at the beginning of the century, with Samuel Butler's *The Way of All Flesh . . .*" (*Two Cheers*, 275). Forster's words apply as well to the naturist heirs of Butler, for they were among the first writers to face the unconscious life with direct awareness. It is a remarkable fact of literary history that during the same years (1890–1922) in which the naturists were searching for an accurate language and a definitive myth of the unconscious, on the Continent a scientist-physician was following a different path toward an analogous goal.

If the urgent need to make contact with "independent worlds of ephemerons" was the source of the naturist adventure, it was also the guiding force behind the achievement of Sigmund Freud. Freud's work constitutes a systematic and reasoned attempt to bridge the same two worlds – the orgiastic outer world of biology and the tragic inner world of spiritual man. For the naturists, that outer world or "landscape" was both the ultimate Darwinian progenitor, the earth-mother, of man, and a mirror for his hidden instinctual life. But Freud looked at the "thing itself," the biological organism. For Freud, the human infant became the primal object of contemplation; the child became father of the man.

Spirit of place, from Hardy to Lawrence, represented a search for the roots of psychic health in terms of the individual's relationship with nature, family, and society at large. Hardy's ephemerons contained the secret of his better world; Ellis's metazoa held the seeds of a new spirit; Butler's "body" was a token of utopia; physical nature offered a promise, for Lawrence, of a real Rananim. This symbolic language contained a twofold signification: it was both a language of the heart, of psychology, and a language of the community, of sociology. So it was with Freud: if psychoanalysis was rooted in the physical processes of the individual animal organism,

Freud recognized that inner world as inseparable from the economic and moral imperatives of society. The progress of Freud's own writings, from *Studies in Hysteria* (1895) to *Civilization and Its Discontents* (1930), indicates his increasing awareness of the radical conflict between biological and social man.

Yet Freud, as scientist, recognized the immense difficulty of obtaining objective conditions for the study of society:

> . . . the diagnosis of communal neurosis is faced with a special difficulty. In an individual neurosis we take as our starting-point the contrast that distinguishes the patient from his environment, which is assumed to be "normal." For a group all of whose members are affected by one and the same disorder no such background could exist; it would have to be found elsewhere.[1]

The literature of place represents a search for Freud's "elsewhere." Each of these works is built upon a journey from an environment of "neurosis" to one of "normality"; each is constructed around an informing vision of the sane or healthy society; each suffers the artistic flaws that result from the struggle to create a background where "no such background could exist." Each of these works is an attempt to face a new challenge: imaginatively to create, through images of *flora* and *fauna*, morphology and topography, a climate of utopia — not in terms of the Platonic philosopher's concept of the Good, but in terms of the biologist-physician's concept of health. Each work is a diagnosis.

In 1890, Ellis had begun to write of sexuality in terms of health and illness rather than good and evil, and had pointed to the unhappiness caused by a repressive moralism. In 1893, Hudson had spoken of "a revelation of an unfamiliar and unsuspected nature hidden under the nature we are conscious of"; he had insisted that "the return to an instinctive or primitive state of mind is accompanied by this feeling of elation, which, in the very young, rises to intense gladness, and sometimes makes them mad with joy like animals newly escaped from captivity"; he had asserted that "the civilized life is one of continual repression" (*Idle Days*, 205).

In 1895, Hardy had sketched, in Sue Bridehead, the portrait of a woman whose sexual inhibitions were clearly related to a pattern of sado-masochism; and in Jude Fawley he had created a character in whom a combination of male and female elements (duly noticed by Lawrence) constituted a new kind of hero in English fiction. In 1896,

Edward Carpenter had joined Ellis in a plea for sexual toleration, and had based his argument upon a biological, rather than a theological, definition of human sexuality.

In 1903 had appeared Butler's classic study of the life-denying repressions which follow in the wake of self-righteous propriety. Butler's Ernest Pontifex had identified guilt as a destroyer: " 'What a fool,' he said, 'a man is to remember anything that happened more than a week ago unless it was pleasant . . .' " (*Way*, 91). In 1904 Hudson had created, in Rima, a symbol of the unreflecting spontaneity which was man's rightful inheritance as a part of the animal kingdom, and had insisted that Rima's "law" took precedence over the "law" of civilization. In 1905 Forster had sketched, in the pattern of Hardy's Sue, a woman whose sexual frustration had found a release symbolized by the phallic towers of Monteriano, but whose death in childbirth seemed a mark of society's vengeance upon the liberated individual. In 1892 Norman Douglas had begun his studies of animal sexuality, a theme which is present in all his works, from *Paneros* through *South Wind*.

Lawrence had already imitated, in his first novel (1911), the teeming sexuality which lay beneath the surfaces of Hardy's descriptions of organic life. In October 1913, after he had finished *Sons and Lovers*, Lawrence had not yet read Freud;[2] but by the time of his next novel, *The Rainbow* (1916), it is clear that he is acquainted with the imagery of Freudianism. Yet the ground had been ploughed for Lawrence's sowing, not by Freud, but by the naturists, for these writers had dealt with themes which anticipated, with a striking accuracy, Freud's formulations. For example, the theme of childhood – along with the related images of "games" and "play" – which took diverse shapes in Butler's *Way of All Flesh*, Hudson's *Green Mansions*, Lawrence's *White Peacock*, and Douglas's *London Street Games*, represents an attempt to express a universal craving for an undifferentiated, amorphous sensuality. It is precisely this instinct for which Freud coined the term "polymorphous perverse."[3] The sudden, irresponsible explosions of Wells's Polly or Lawrence's Birkin, the ritual games of Hudson's Rima and Kipling's Kim, the elaborate hobby-horses of Butler's Ernest Pontifex or Douglas's Count Caloviglia, the sensuous horse-play of Forster's Gino or Lawrence's Cicio – all are evocations of the sensuous freedom of the Freudian infant. The desire for release from what Lawrence calls "the terrible bondage of this tick-tack of time" (*Women*, 456), an impulse which we have traced through Hardy and Hudson, Tomlinson and Wells, is a counterpart to the Freudian doctrine that "in the id there is nothing corresponding to the idea of time."[4]

Freud's attention to the mundane animal needs parallels a renewal of literary interest in what the Count, in *South Wind*, calls "healthy animals": the physical magnetism of Walter Morel, toasting his breakfast bacon in the fireplace; or the animal stability of Joyce's Leopold Bloom, burning his breakfast kidney over the coals, or ruminating as he defecates at Number Seven Eccles Street. Wells's Polly is indeed a digestive barometer: his over-eating problem disappears when he is liberated from Mrs. Polly and takes up a pastoral life. This renewed interest in animality was part of a strain of primitivism among the naturist writers. But the foundations of Freud's own work are deeply primitivistic, beginning, as they did, with studies of atavistic states of hysteria. For Freud, as for Lawrence, "where the individual begins, life begins"; but the individual is "inconceivable," and "the unconscious is never an abstraction, *never to be abstracted.*"[5] Freud and the naturists, in their diverse ways, struggled to create a language of the unconscious.

An account of the naturist movement is indeed a story of the discontents of civilization; and Freud's book of that title provides an appropriate conclusion to the tale. We can do no better, in fact, than to allow Freud to summarize for us, in passages from *Civilization and Its Discontents*, the naturist message.

In spite of the prevailing image of Freud as a "pessimist," there is ample evidence that Freud shared the guarded optimism of the naturists. He insisted that the "dispute within the libido . . . does admit of an eventual accommodation in the individual, as, it may be hoped, it will also do in the future of civilization, however much that civilization may oppress the life of the individual today" (88). Though Freud objected to socialist idealism, he confirmed the fundamental tenet of Marxism: "I too think it quite certain that a real change in the relations of human beings to possessions would be of more help . . . than any ethical commands . . ." (90). It is appropriate that Freud's favorite writer among the Edwardians was John Galsworthy (52), whose special work it was to portray the enervating effects of the modern worship of property. Freud's conviction was part of the naturist view, from Ellis through Lawrence.

The idea of Eros as a source of social cohesion, which Ellis and Carpenter inherited in part from Whitman, was part of a general naturist emphasis upon sexual love as a fundament of social health. Freud shared this conviction: ". . . civilization is a process in the service of Eros, whose purpose it is to combine single human individuals, and after that families, then races, peoples and nations, into one great unity, the unity of mankind. . . . These collections of men are to be libidinally bound to one another" (69). Hardy's advocacy of a "society divided into *groups of temperaments*, with a different code of observances for each group," a view shared by Butler, Douglas, Ellis, and Forster, was echoed by Freud: the social requirement "that there shall be a single kind of sexual life for everyone, disregards the dissimilarities, whether innate or acquired, in the sexual constitution of human beings; it cut off a fair number of them from sexual enjoyment, and so becomes the source of a serious injustice" (51).

The central message of *Civilization and Its Discontents* is Freud's identification, in the spirit of Butler, Hardy, and Douglas, of "the sense of guilt as the most important problem in the development of civilization . . . the price we pay for our advance in civilization is a loss of happiness through the heightening of the sense of guilt" (81). And when Freud predicted a new science, "a pathology of cultural communities" (91), we inevitably recall the "college of Spiritual pathology" which occupied Ernest Pontifex's attention at the end of *The Way of All Flesh*.

Butler's bitter concern with the questionable motivation of Christian moralists – a concern shared by Douglas and Forster – reappeared in Freud: "Every renunciation of instinct now becomes a dynamic source of conscience and every fresh renunciation increases the latter's severity and intolerance" (75). The Hardy of *Tess* and *Jude* would passionately concur with Freud that "the liberty of the individual is no gift of civilization" (42); Hardy might have recognized Freud's concise diagnosis of the case of Sue Bridehead: "When an instinctual trend undergoes repression, its libidinal elements are turned into symptoms, and its aggressive components into a sense of guilt" (86). Tomlinson would agree with Freud that "civilization is built upon a renunciation of instinct" (44); and Hudson might well have applauded Freud's contention that "what we call our civilization is largely responsible for our misery," and that "we should be much happier if we gave it up and returned to primitive conditions" (33).

The naturist travel-novelists might have accepted Freud's remark that "order is a kind of compulsion to repeat" (40) as a defense of their revolt against the "order" of traditional plot devices. And Lawrence might have found support for his contention that "the picture is the death" in Freud's own doubts: ". . . how far we are from mastering the characteristics of mental life by representing them in pictorial terms" (18).

Lawrence's attack, in *Women in Love*, upon the Baconian victory over nature, found confirmation in the self-doubts of the modern Baconian, Freud: ". . . this subjugation of the forces of nature . . . has not made man feel happier" (35). And the Lawrentian opposition between "law" and "love", consciousness and organism, was a counterpart to Freud's two fundamental and opposing instinctual principles: love and death. Freud emphasized "man's discovery that sexual (genital) love afforded him the strongest experience of satisfaction, and in fact provided him with the prototype of all happiness" (48). Lawrence would surely have agreed.

It seems appropriate that *Civilization and Its Discontents* was published in the same year (1930) in which D. H. Lawrence died. A more fitting epitaph could not have been composed, nor a more eloquent summary of the naturist message. Freud surely expressed the major claim of this group of writers, from Hardy through Lawrence, when he suggested, in a letter to a friend, that "I have always confined myself to the ground floor and the basement of the edifice."[6] For Freud and the naturists placed the human animal in a new world, a world without the intellectual ladders of humanism or Christianity; a world in which each man must descend to "the things themselves" in order to find himself; a world described by Yeats in "The Circus Animals' Desertion":

> Now that my ladder's gone,
> I must lie down where all the ladders start,
> In the foul rag-and-bone shop of the heart.

8 Epilogue: Is Great Pan Dead?

> There is an objective world, a chaos, a cinder heap. . . . A land-
> scape, with occasional oases. . . . But mainly deserts of dirt,
> ash-pits of the cosmos, grass on ash-pits.
>
> T. E. Hulme, *Speculations*

This landscape might be taken as the epitaph of the naturist movement. Hulme's brilliant but uneven essay, compiled from notebooks
which remained after his death in combat (1917), is significant as
a landmark of change far outweighing its intrinsic merit. *Speculations*
(1924) is symptomatic of the emergence of a new art based upon old
values, those of classicism and traditional religious dogma. Hulme
recognized that this modern revolt would be based on a radical
change in taste and outlook: the final chapter of his book is titled
"Cinders: A New Weltanschauung." Hulme's new "world-view"
totally rejected the spirit of vitalism and organicism which permeates
the art of our civilization from the Renaissance through the Romantics to naturism. Hulme reserves special scorn for those he calls
"the Naturalists," whom he condemns for "taking physical science as
the only possible type of real knowledge."[1]

If Darwin set the naturist adventure in motion with his voyage
on the *Beagle*, sailing to Tierra del Fuego, Hulme might be said to
have brought the movement to an end with his essay on sailing to
Byzantium. For it was in the hard geometry of Byzantine mosaics that
Hulme found the pattern for the new art of the twentieth century.
"The new art," he wrote, "is geometrical in character, while the art
we are accustomed to is vital and organic" (77).

The geometrical intensity cherished by Hulme reflected the same
powerful cultural revolt which had already taken shape in the paintings of the Post-Impressionists, and especially the Cubists. Much of
the impetus for the movement came from Cézanne, in whose paint-

ings the geological and biological shapes of the naturist landscapes began to be reduced to the cones, cubes, globes, pyramids, and cylinders which became the idiom of Cubism. Though Cézanne believed he was uncovering essential shapes beneath the appearance of nature, with Cubism this impulse constituted in fact the victory of geometry over nature which Hulme recommended. Paris was the shrine of the new movement, and all the arts were affected. In sculpture, Brancusi erected massive inert stone blocks; Epstein's angular statues provided inspiration for Hulme himself, just as Gaudier-Brzeska's abstract forms became an informing spirit for the early poetry of Ezra Pound. The same spirit breathed in the early ballet scores of Stravinsky, whose spare orchestration and sharply disjointed rhythms and dissonances constituted acts of defiance aimed at the swelling, organic, and seamless harmonies of father Wagner; or in the quieter piano pieces of Erik Satie, whose exact and mechanical formality again countered Wagner, and seemed to announce (not without humor) the advent of a mathematical age.

Thus Hulme was not unique in his advocacy of these ideas. The special value of Hulme's book for the historian of ideas results from his dramatic and dogmatic confrontation with the spirit of naturism. Hulme is a young man in revolt. Where Darwin and his disciples had found in nature a wisdom superior to the thoughts of men, Hulme insists that "nature is the accumulation of the memories of man" (225). Where Lawrence protests that nature is not "scenery," Hulme cryptically notes: "Nature. Scenery as built up by man. Oases in the desert of grit" (225). If the naturists saw the operation of natural laws as independent of human thought, Hulme, prefiguring Sartre, declares that "truths don't exist before we invent them" (240). And where the naturists found order in organic life, Hulme sees dust and ashes: "There is difficulty in finding a comprehensive scheme of the cosmos, because there is none. The cosmos is only organised in parts; the rest is cinders" (220).

This landscape of cinders, these "deserts of dirt, ash-pits of the cosmos," provide the first glimpse of the environment of the new art. For this is the setting of *The Waste Land*, the model poem for the coming age, composed by Hulme's most talented and influential disciple, T. S. Eliot, who along with Ezra Pound had absorbed Hulme's ideas long before the publication of *Speculations*. In Eliot's poem, the naturist landscape – the place of hope and rejuvenation – is replaced by the cinder-heap that provides the characteristic setting of the literature of our time:

What are the roots that clutch, what branches grow
Out of this stony rubbish? Son of man,
You cannot say, or guess, for you know only
A heap of broken images, where the sun beats,
And the dead tree gives no shelter, the cricket no relief,
And the dry stone no sound of water.

The Waste Land was published in the year 1922; the same year saw the Paris publication of James Joyce's *Ulysses*, which would become as important a pattern for the novel as *The Waste Land* would be for poetry. In Joyce's novel, the green world of the naturists is gone (except as memory), and in its place a Dublin landscape of streets and culs-de-sac, bars, and offices. Again Hulme's essay is prophetic: his hard imagistic style seems often to evoke with uncanny precision both the method and the content of Joyce's world. Hulme writes: "Walking in the street, seeing pretty girls (all chaos put into the drains: not seen) and wondering what they would look like ill. Men laughing at a bar – but wait till the fundamental chaos reveals itself" (227).

For Hulme, this "fundamental chaos" permeates the world; the only oases in Hulme's desert are works of art. Thus if the naturists follow Darwin in his insistence upon the superiority of biological life over art, Hulme announces the counter-creed which has gained wide acceptance among artists and academics in our age: the superiority of art over life. (T. S. Eliot was an exception; he considered this belief in the autonomy of art a modern form of idol-worship.) The creed was not new; its genealogy can be traced back through Wilde, Pater, and Ruskin to Flaubert's art of "contre-création" (to use Sartre's phrase), the creation of an alternative artifact superior to the flawed one presumably produced by God. Thus when Stephen Dedalus concludes that "after God, Shakespeare created most," we have little doubt which of the creations he prefers.

The Waste Land and *Ulysses*, both composed of chaotic fragments brought into aesthetic unity, both complex and intricately structured, both built upon scaffoldings of ancient myth, prefigure an art wherein the death of God in the nineteeth century is brought to completion by the death of nature in the twentieth. Eliot's dead tree that "gives no shelter" will reappear in the *mis en scène* of Samuel Beckett's

Waiting for Godot: "A country road. A tree," and in *Endgame*, Hamm will remark that "Outside of here, it's death." "Nature has forgotten us," he complains, and Clov replies with finality: "There's no more nature."

Nor is there much nature in the major fiction of the last sixty years. In Kafka's works, natural phenomena serve as expressionistic extensions of our inner anguish – the horse and the snowstorm, for example, in "The Country Doctor"; Proust's magnificent naturist visions of childhood splendors in the grass and young girls among flowers turn out to be, in their recapture, cruel deceptions. Hemingway admits a debt to naturism: "I learned from D. H. Lawrence how to describe country," he once remarked to his brother;[2] but eventually his characters find in nature only a fleeting refuge from their painful liaisons, and Hemingway's natural setting inevitably becomes a stage for the predatory activities of men who hunt, fish, or fight each other for release. Among the characters of Faulkner, Dilsey's quiet strength and endurance seems to spring from a world of physical nature, but for the rest Faulkner's dusty landscape offers, like Eliot's cricket, no relief. In the novels of Fitzgerald, and later those of Mailer and Bellow, nature seems to have been totally obliterated within an urban sensibility.

After D. H. Lawrence, the novel in English would turn away from its indigenous naturist heritage and float like a stream of consciousness along the various international currents of symbolism, expressionism, naturalism, imagism, occultism, futurism, surrealism, absurdism, and the tradition of the new. Virginia Woolf's rather astounding remark that "on or about December 1910 human nature changed" (she is here referring specifically to the first London exhibition of Post-Impressionist paintings) serves to remind us that it was precisely at this time that the works of Eliot and Joyce, Proust and Kafka were germinating, and that naturism began its decline. Perhaps Virginia Woolf's arbitrary date will serve as well as any for the beginning of the demise of Pan. To be sure, it was in precisely the same month (December 1910) that D. H. Lawrence received an advance copy of his first novel, *The White Peacock*, and was at work on his first mature novel, *Sons and Lovers*. But Lawrence, after all, was the last voice of naturism, which would disappear as a literary movement after another decade.

Critics and teachers of literature would play a crucial role in this broad change of taste recommended by Hulme and his followers. With the rise of the New Criticism in the 1940s, art seemed subtly to be valued above life, and the complexity of a work of art became in some way a token of its worth as a mirror held up to a complex age. Thus the attribution of literary excellence became dependent upon the complex critical webs that could be woven around a story or a poem. Donne's poetry was usually preferred to Spenser's, Marvell's to Milton's, Hopkins's to Hardy's. Conrad's stories were found to be more interesting than Hardy's, and Joyce was thought to be superior to Lawrence. It was felt that if this new and clever critical machinery could not be successfully utilized in response to a poem or novel, the work itself must be wanting in art. The presence of symbol and myth, creating simultaneously several levels of meaning, was sought out and prized by critics and students. Ambiguity was often mistaken for breadth of insight, irony for profundity, richness of cultural allusion for wisdom. A novel such as *Green Mansions*, which was the most popular novel of the Edwardian decade, seemed absurd and even silly to critics who admired the rich ironies of Conrad and Joyce. Indeed it was the comparative absence of irony in naturist literature that seemed to make it so ill-suited to our enigmatic and problematic age. The feeling seemed to be that the naive and simplistic optimism of these nature-lovers had been discredited by the ugly facts of twentieth-century history.

All art must reduce and distort in order to organize and intensify; but if it is not to become deliberate mystification, art must maintain a balance between the claims of nature and those of "geometry." Modern story-telling devices such as "scrambled time," "stream-of-consciousness," and multiple points of view, interrupt the flow of outer events and then reconstruct them in order to achieve concentration and intensity. But the events, and the natural world in which they occur, remain caught in subjectivity and enigma. Conrad, Ford, Joyce, and Faulkner recognized and demonstrated that subjectivity is always enigmatic; they knew the power of enigma. But the price they paid was that ambiguity tyrannizes over their art. Chaucer's tales provide ample proof that irony and ambiguity are not incompatible with a deep respect for the order in nature, and T. S. Eliot knew the abyss that lay between Chaucer's opening line ("Whan that Aprill with his shoures soote") and his own ("April is the cruellest month"). Shakespeare constructed in *Macbeth* and *Hamlet* convincing labyrinths of confusion and despair without neglecting what Samuel Johnson called "general nature." The same might be said of *Wuthering Heights, Jane Eyre, The Mill on the Floss,* and *Tess of the d'Urbervilles.* Our admiration for the power of a story must be tempered by an awareness of what has been left out in order to achieve that power.

For Hulme it mattered not if the whole cosmos were omitted, for the cosmos was "cinders." The naturists would not be alone in objecting that this is an enormous price to pay for the stimulus of "intensity."

Cultural historians may find that the hallmark of literature in the age of Yeats, Joyce, Eliot, and Pound has been the rage for formal synthesis, the need to wring, at whatever price, an artistic order out of the torn pieces of our malaise. Few can doubt the Daedalian cunning of these artists, or the beauty of the works they have made. Yet to have designed, as Daedalus did, a perfect labyrinth, is an achievement of considerable ambivalence, and for this success a price may have been paid, a crucial presence may have been ignored. When Georg Lukács suggests that "the desire for synthesis . . . turns in a circle; it is the subjective expression of the *circulus vitiosus* of modern bourgeois art and culture,"[3] we are likely to think of the gyres, cycles, spirals, and circles which govern the structures of *Ulysses*, "Byzantium," *The Pisan Cantos*, and *The Four Quartets*. These works constitute, among other things, attempts to escape the net of personal subjectivity by means of intricate and tightly wrought form; but Lukács insists that such formalism remains only a symptom of the "subjectivity" of the decaying culture itself. Where Hulme sees and aesthetic order wrested from natural cinders, Lukács, quoting Ernst Bloch, sees a natural order reduced to aesthetic cinders: "Writers of significance can no longer find the way into their material except by smashing it," and the result is only "some mixable rubble."[4]

Lukács' devastating censure is a reminder that he is perhaps as unfair in his condemnation of these admirable works of art as T. E. Hulme is unfair to the insights of naturism. But Lukács does recognize, as Lawrence did, that the crucial problem for the modern artist is the trap of self-consciousness; and his comments may serve to indicate to us that the sources of liberation may not be present within the culture itself. " 'Did I feel a twinge in my little toe or didn't I' asks every character of Mr. Joyce or of Miss Richardson or M. Proust," Lawrence complained. "It is self-consciousness, picked into such fine bits that the bits . . . are invisible. . . . And there's the serious novel: senile-precocious. Absorbedly, childishly concerned with *what I am*. I am this, I am that, I am the other. My reactions are such, and such, and such."[5]

This is the disease of Eliot's Prufrock and Joyce's Stephen and Bloom, of Kafka's K and Proust's Marcel, and they all bespeak a terrible truth about us. But when these characters are set within larger frameworks of narrative form and broader contexts of history and myth, when they are portrayed with the immediacy of a spare, direct, and concise prose style, do we then see them "in perspective"? Do these characters and the narratives of which they are a part then assume the objectivity of life seen steadily and seen whole? Does "the twinge in my little toe" then appear for what it really is in this vast universe? Lawrence thought not: something was missing. Virginia Woolf points to the same omission: ". . . did not the reading of *Ulysses* suggest how much of life is excluded or ignored, and did it not come with a shock to open *Tristram Shandy* or even *Pendennis* and be by them convinced that there are not only other aspects of life, but more important ones into the bargain."[6]

Joyce and Eliot knew that the subjective view is only the effect of selective cultural conditioning upon the individual; it is less clear that they saw culture, in turn, as nothing but the same subjectivity multiplied and played back upon the culture itself. Sartre, Camus, Beckett, Genet, and countless other artists and philosophers have churned about in this neo-Cartesian dilemma, but the problem of the chicken and the egg remains, as does our society, caught in solipsism. To many critics, it seems that modern art has nowhere to look for regeneration outside itself: a dying culture apparently must nurse itself back to health. There is, of course, no dearth of "answers" to this problem: Lukács himself doubtless recommends Marxism, Eliot Christianity, and Pound a kind of cross-cultural eclecticism. To each the naturist would respond that these remedies are all put together by thought, fabricated out of the sick culture itself, and therefore bound to be subtly infected with the same contagion. "Most men die," says a character in Molière, "not of their maladies, but of their remedies"; and the naturist would add that the same is true of societies and civilizations. The naturist contends that sources of health and sanity *do* exist; but that they have their existence in a world "beyond culture" – although the naturist would perhaps alter Lionel Trilling's useful phrase to read "*beneath* culture." For they believed, with Rousseau and Freud, that the freedom of the individual is not a gift of civilization, and exists prior to culture, not because of it. "We reflect," Trilling writes, "that somewhere in the child, somewhere in the adult, there is a hard, irreducible, stubborn core of biological urgency, and biological necessity, and biological *reason*, that culture

E

cannot reach and that reserves the right, which sooner or later it will exercise, to judge the culture and resist and reverse it."[7]

Powers and functions which in the past were attributed to God, or to the gods, or to some unknowable divine ground in nature, are today the province of the sciences, technologies, philosophies, works of art, and other structures put together by the human mind. We may doubt how well humans have succeeded in this god-like task. Montaigne wrote, four hundred years ago: "We have abandoned nature and presume to give lessons to her who used to guide us so happily and surely." And Horace warned, two thousand years ago: "You may drive out nature with a fork, but she will always return."

From the beginning, the European novel was written for readers who were no longer very interested in nature; they were fascinated rather by the workings of society. This examination of bourgeois life and manners has been the special subject of the novel from *Moll Flanders* and *Tom Jones* to *Bleak House* and *The Great Gatsby*. For this critique we are thankful; but we have cause to suspect that the portrait is now fairly complete. Times, places, technologies have changed, but the hunger for money, power, and status in the urban exchange is hardly different from what it was in the age of Balzac or Thackeray. *Plus ça change, plus c'est la même chose.* The novelist's catalogue of status-objects and possessions may change, but this is of no importance, as Virginia Woolf remarks about the "materialist" fiction of Bennett, Galsworthy, and Wells: ". . . they write of unimportant things . . . they spend immense skill and immense industry making the trivial and the transitory appear the true and the enduring."[8] What is missing from these novels, she adds, is what is most important in our life: "Life escapes; and perhaps without life nothing else is worth while. . . . Whether we call it life or spirit, truth or reality, this, the essential thing, has moved off, or on, and refuses to be contained any longer in such ill-fitting vestments as we provide."

What is this "life" that escapes? Woolf admits the difficulty of locating or identifying this "essential thing," and resorts to a memorable but elusive metaphor: "Life is a luminous halo." But her questions remain crucial in our time: "Is life like this? Must novels be like this?" The naturists answered these questions directly and unequivocally: "life" is the cosmos of which human beings are a part; life is what goes on of its own accord, without the willful interventions of men. This given natural world is the only ground from which we can gain perspective upon our civilization; it is our only source of sanity. The naturists would argue that our disregard for this ground of life is the cause both of the spoliation of our planet and of the sterility of our art.

Like all of us, the modern novelist, in his preoccupation with the terrifying existential drama, typically neglects the stage on which it takes place. If he notices this background of nature, he tends to see it only as an extension of human thought, a catalyst for desire, an object for manipulation. The over-specialized English and American novel, if it is to renew its vitality, must turn back to the tradition out of which it grew – a tradition of exuberant and unshakeable faith in the workings of the world of nature which constitutes the unique genius of English literature from Chaucer and Shakespeare to the Romantics and naturists. For naturism is, after all, only the latest – and hopefully not the last – transmutation within a great native tradition. It is this broad and enduring tradition which Hardy and Forster have in mind when they evoke the presence of Celtic survivals at Stonehenge or Cadbury Ring, or when they remind us of the geological time which makes both clock time and psychological time possible. It is this tradition to which the naturists allude when they describe themselves as descendants of Erasmus, Montaigne, and Rabelais, or when they place their characters, even after the Fall, in surviving pastures and bosques of Eden.

Fifty years ago, D. H. Lawrence called for just such a return to our indigenous roots in such essays as "Pan in America" and "Surgery for the Novel – or a Bomb." Joyce indeed provided a bomb, and perhaps this fragmentation will prove to have been a salutary event, like Birkin's stoning of the reflection of the moon. Lawrence saw that if "great Pan is dead," then the English novel too was dying. But he was aware, as Nietzsche had been, that reports of the death of Pan were a bit premature. If Pan was dead in civilization, he was still alive in nature: "In the days before man got too much separated off from the universe, he *was* Pan, along with all the rest. As a tree still is."⁹ In *The Longest Journey* – which was among other things an answer to the Socratic question, "is the cow there?" – Forster is concerned to assure us that, yes, after all, "the cow *is* there." Lawrence and Forster are affirming, in their different ways, that Great Pan indeed lives on, and that Hulme's ash-pits and cinders are not in the macro-cosmos inhabited by Pan, but in the micro-cosmos projected by the human mind.

"Let it be confessed," wrote Rainer Maria Rilke, "landscape is foreign to us, and we are fearfully alone, amongst trees which blossom and by streams which flow."[10] Yet even Rilke's trees and streams have slowly disappeared as the modern novel has turned to the city-scapes of Waugh's London, Joyce's Dublin, Durrell's Alexandria, Henry Miller's Paris, the Los Angeles of Isherwood and the Chicagos and Clevelands of Dreiser, Dos Passos, Farrell, and Bellow. Baudelaire's "fourmillante cité" and Eliot's "unreal city" provide our literature with its machine-produced scenery. And why not, it will be asked, since we live increasingly in just such an urban, man-fabricated environment?

The response of the naturists, from Hardy to Lawrence, would be unanimous and decisive, though it might surprise us; for they would assure us that, after all their talk about spirit of place, naturism finally has nothing to do with "going to the country." From the beginning, landscape had been for the naturist an outer correlative for an inner state of awareness; always their spirit of place was a physical presence only in order that it might embody and express a consciousness of unity. The most trenchant statement of the naturist faith is the aphorism of Henri-Fréderic Amiel: "Un paysage quelconque est un état de l'âme" ("Any landscape is a condition of the spirit").

William Carlos Williams was right, in his poem "Raleigh was Right":

> We cannot go to the country
> for the country will bring us no peace
> What can the small violets tell us
> that grow on furry stems in
> the long grass among lance shaped leaves?

The issue is whether the condition of spirit reflected in naturist literature can be realized within the outer setting of the city-scape. It is quite true that the twentieth-century city physically mirrors the tormented spirit of its inhabitants. But it might be noticed that William Carlos Williams has himself caught the spirit of Lawrence and the naturists; he has found and evoked a naturist consciousness in the unlikely industrial landscape of Paterson, New Jersey. Thus the poets and novelists of our time are left with a question which is perhaps the final legacy of naturist literature: if we cannot go to the country, then can we bring the spirit of the country to the very heart of the city? For ultimately the naturist adventure was about the power and the immensity of the unknown. Can we learn again to allow the unknown to touch the known?

There is an ancient story of a wise monk who one day appeared before his disciples in a great hall to deliver a discourse. As he was about to begin, a bird alighted on a window-sill and began to sing. The great hall was filled with bird-song; the monk and his students listened in silence; the bird finished its singing and flew away. Thereupon the monk abruptly dismissed his disciples saying, "The sermon is over."

Notes

CHAPTER 1 HARDY: A BETTER WORLD

1 "Study of Thomas Hardy," *Phoenix: The Posthumous Papers of D. H. Lawrence*, ed. Edward D. McDonald (New York, 1936) p. 480.
2 Joseph Warren Beach, *The Technique of Thomas Hardy* (New York, 1962) p. 174.
3 Preface to 5th (English) ed., *Tess of the d'Urbervilles* (London, 1910) p. x. Citations from Hardy's novels in my text are to the Harper Thin-Paper Edition of 1910, unless otherwise indicated.
4 *Letters of W. B. Yeats*, ed. Allan Wade (New York, 1955) p. 922.
5 *The Second Common Reader* (New York, 1960) p. 225.
6 *Two Cheers for Democracy* (New York, 1951) p. 275.
7 *Apocalypse* (New York, 1966) p. 223.
8 New York and London, 1965, pp. 1–2.
9 *The Descent of Man* (New York and London, 1871) II, 186.
10 *On the Origin of Species by means of Natural Selection* (London, 1911) p. 75.
11 Ibid., p. 102.
12 Ibid., p. 100.
13 *The Descent of Man*, p. 386.
14 "A Literary Transference," *The Southern Review*, Hardy Centennial Number (VI, 1940), in *Hardy: A Collection of Critical Essays*, ed. Albert J. Guerard (Englewood Cliffs, N.J., 1963) p. 139.
15 Florence Emily Hardy, *The Life of Thomas Hardy 1840–1928* (New York, 1962) p. 234.
16 Havelock Ellis, *The New Spirit*, 3rd ed. (London, 1892) p. xv.
17 Havelock Ellis, "Thomas Hardy's Novels," *Westminster Review*, CXIX (1 June 1883) 362.
18 *Psychoanalysis and the Unconscious and Fantasia of the Unconscious* (New York, 1960) p. 83.
19 *Thomas Henry Huxley* (Edinburgh and London, 1905) p. 112.
20 *Ernest Pontifex or The Way of All Flesh*, ed. Daniel F. Howard (New York, 1964) p. 178.
21 *The Varieties of Religious Experience: A Study in Human Nature* (New York, 1902) p. 206.
22 Beach, *Technique*, p. 236.
23 Tennyson, *In Memoriam A. H. H.*, ll. 1059–60.
24 Norman Douglas, *South Wind* (New York, 1960) p. 167.

25 Albert J. Guerard, *Thomas Hardy: The Novels and Stories* (New York, 1964) p. 62.
26 Cited by Morton Dauwen Zabel, "Hardy in Defense of His Art: The Aesthetic of Incongruity," in Guerard, *Essays*, p. 31.

CHAPTER 2 BUTLER: THE NEW SPIRIT

1 Ellis, "Hardy's Novels," p. 337.
2 Havelock Ellis, *My Life* (Boston, 1939) p. 191.
3 Ellis, *New Spirit*, p. 1.
4 "The Experimental Novel," in *The Modern Tradition: Backgrounds of Modern Literature*, ed. Richard Ellmann and Charles Feidelson, Jr. (New York, 1964) p. 289.
5 *Love's Coming of Age*, 12th ed. (London, 1923) p. 32.
6 Cited by Carpenter, *Love's Coming*, p. 66.
7 Cited in *Twentieth Century Authors*, ed. Stanley J. Kunitz and Howard Haycroft (New York, 1942) p. 682.
8 Cited by A. F. Tschiffely, *Don Roberto* (London, 1937) p. 265.
9 Ibid., p. 266.
10 *Far Away and Long Ago* (New York, 1923) p. 342. Citations from Hudson will be from this collected edition, unless otherwise indicated.
11 Tschiffely, *Don Roberto*, p. 284.
12 H. M. Tomlinson, *The Sea and the Jungle* (New York, 1961) p. 143.
13 D. G. Hogarth, *The Life of Charles M. Doughty* (London, 1929) p. 3.
14 Cited by Antonina Valentin, *H. G. Wells: Phrophet of Our Day* (New York, 1950) pp. 313–14.
15 See Cecil Woolf, *A Bibliography of Norman Douglas* (London, 1954) pp. 19–24.
16 Grant Allen, *Charles Darwin* (New York, 1893) p. v.
17 Samuel Butler, *Erewhon* (New York, 1961) p. 176.
18 *Two Cheers for Democracy*, p. 220.
19 René Descartes, *Discours de la Méthode* (Paris, 1948) p. 116.
20 Thomas More, *Utopia*, ed. H. V. S. Ogden (New York, 1949) p. 48.

CHAPTER 3 SPIRIT OF PLACE: THE TRAVEL BOOK

1 *Alps and Sanctuaries* (London, 1923) p. 63.
2 *The Voyage of the Beagle* (London, 1906) p. 484.
3 *Idle Days in Patagonia*, p. 4.
4 *Old Calabria* (London, 1938) p. 460.
5 *Etruscan Places* (London, 1956) p. 50. Citations in my text from Lawrence's novels and travel books are to the collected Phoenix Edition (London, 1954–6) unless otherwise indicated.
6 "E. T." (pseud. for Jessie Chambers), *D. H. Lawrence: A Personal Record* (New York, 1965) p. 119.
7 H. M. Tomlinson, *Norman Douglas*, 2nd ed. (London, 1952) p. 12.
8 Charles M. Doughty, Preface to 2nd ed., *Travels in Arabia Deserta*, 9th ed., 2 vols. (London, 1924) I, vii.
9 Norman Douglas, *Experiments* (New York, 1925) pp. 8–9.

10 In *The Portable Conrad,* ed. Morton Dauwen Zabel (New York, 1947) p. 495.
11 "Bavarian Gentians," *The Complete Poems of D. H. Lawrence,* ed. Vivian de Sola Pinto and Warren Roberts, 2 vols. (New York, 1964) II, 697.

CHAPTER 4 SPIRIT OF PLACE: THE NOVEL
1 New York, 1920, p. 18.
2 Preface, *The Nigger of the 'Narcissus,'* in Zabel, *Portable Conrad,* p. 707.
3 See facsimile of title page, from the MS. in the British Museum, in *The Way of All Flesh* (New York, 1925) p. xii.
4 H. G. Wells, *The History of Mr. Polly,* ed. Gordon N. Ray (New York, 1960) p. 184.
5 W. H. Hudson, *Green Mansions* (New York, 1962) p. 83.
6 Chambers, *Record,* p. 122.
7 *153 Letters from W. H. Hudson,* ed. Edward Garnett (New York, 1923) p. 116.
8 Tomlinson, *Douglas,* p. 60.
9 *Howards End* (New York, 1944) p. 33.
10 *The Longest Journey* (New York, 1922) p. 55.
11 *A Passage to India* (New York, 1924) p. 225.
12 H. G. Wells, "Jude the Obscure," *Saturday Review,* 8 Feb. 1896, p. 154; cited by Ray, *Mr. Polly,* p. xii.

CHAPTER 5 HARDY AND LAWRENCE
1 *The Letters of D. H. Lawrence,* ed. Aldous Huxley (London, 1932) p. 208.
2 Cited by Harry T. Moore, *The Intelligent Heart: The Story of D. H. Lawrence* (New York, 1954) p. 223.
3 "Study," *Phoenix,* p. 398.
4 Huxley, Introduction, *Letters,* p. xxx.
5 Chambers, *Record,* p. 179.
6 New York, 1960, pp. 226–36.
7 New York, 1962, p. 173.
8 Moore, *Intelligent Heart,* p. 216.
9 Huxley, *Letters,* p. 197.
10 *Fantasia,* p. 164.

CHAPTER 6 LAWRENCE: A VERSION OF PASTORAL
1 Quoted in *The Essential T. E. Lawrence,* ed. David Garnett (London, 1951) p. 278.
2 "Vorticism," in Ellman and Feildelson, *Modern Tradition,* p. 151.
3 Huxley, *Letters,* pp. 111–12.
4 Cited by F. O. Matthiessen, *American Renaissance* (New York, 1941) p. 616.
5 *Myth and the English Mind from Piers Plowman to Edward Gibbon* (New York, 1961) p. 616.
6 "Making Love to Music," *Sex, Literature, and Censorship,* ed. Harry T. Moore (New York, 1959) p. 45.
7 New York, 1961, p. 248.

F

CHAPTER 7 TOWARD FREUD

1 Sigmund Freud, *Civilization and Its Discontents*, trans. James Strachey New York, 1961) p. 91.
2 See Frederick J. Hoffman, *Freudianism and the Literary Mind* (New York, 1959) pp. 151–76, and Moore, *Intelligent Heart*, pp. 176–7.
3 *A General Introduction to Psycho-Analysis*, trans. J. Rivière (New York, 1953) pp. 332–7.
4 *Collected Papers*, ed. J. Rivière and J. Strachey, 5 vols. (New York and London, 1924–50) v, 119.
5 Lawrence, *Psychoanalysis and the Unconscious*, p. 42.
6 Cited by Ludwig Binswanger, *Sigmund Freud: Reminiscences of a Friendship* (New York, 1957) p. 99.

CHAPTER 8 EPILOGUE: IS GREAT PAN DEAD?

1 New York, n.d., p. 21.
2 Leicester Hemingway, *My Brother, Ernest Hemingway* (Cleveland, 1962) p. 171.
3 *Essays on Thomas Mann* (New York, 1964) pp. 69–70.
4 Ibid., p. 102.
5 "Surgery for the Novel – or a Bomb," *Phoenix*, p. 517.
6 "Modern Fiction," *The Common Reader* (New York, 1953) p. 156.
7 *Beyond Culture* (New York, 1965) p. 115.
8 *Common Reader*, p. 153.
9 "Pan in America," *Phoenix*, p. 24.
10 "Worpswede," *Selected Works*, trans. G. Craig Houston (London, 1954) p. 7.

Bibliography

Aldington, Richard. *Portrait of a Genius, But* . . . London, 1950.
Allen, Grant. *Charles Darwin.* New York, 1893.
—— *et al. Nature Studies.* London, 1882.
Allen, Walter. *The English Novel: A Short Critical History.* New York, 1954.
—— *The Modern Novel.* New York, 1965.
Auden, W. H. "A Literary Transference," *Southern Review*, vi (summer 1940) 78–86.
Babbitt, Irving. *Rousseau and Romanticism.* Boston and New York, 1919.
Bailey, J. O. *Thomas Hardy and the Cosmic Mind: A New Reading of the Dynasts.* New York, 1956.
Baker, Carlos. "The Source-Book for Hudson's *Green Mansions*," *PMLA*, xli (1946) 252–7.
Barrett, William. *Irrational Man.* New York, 1958.
Bates, H. E. "Joseph Conrad and Thomas Hardy," *The English Novelists*, ed. Derek Verschoyle. London, 1936.
Beach, Joseph Warren. *The Technique of Thomas Hardy.* New York, 1962.
—— *The Twentieth Century Novel: Studies in Technique.* New York, 1932.
Beer, John B. *The Achievement of E. M. Forster.* New York, 1962.
Bennett, Arnold. *The Old Wives' Tale.* New York, 1963.
Bergonzi, Bernard. *The Early H. G. Wells.* Manchester, 1961.
Bissell, Claude T. "A Study of The Way of All Flesh," *Nineteenth Century Studies*, ed. R. C. Bald *et al.* Ithaca, N.Y., 1940.
Block, Haskell M. "James Joyce and Thomas Hardy," *MLQ*, xix (Dec 1958) 337–42.
Blunt, Wilfrid Scawen. *My Diaries: Being a Personal Narrative of Events 1888–1914.* 2 vols. New York, 1923.
Brown, Norman O. *Life Against Death: The Psychoanalytic Meaning of History.* New York, 1959.
Butler, Samuel. *Alps and Sanctuaries of Piedmont and the Canton of Ticino*, ed. Henry Festing Jones and A. T. Bartholomew. London, 1923 (Shrewsbury Edition).
—— *Erewhon.* New York, 1961.
—— *Life and Habit*, ed. Henry Festing Jones and A. T. Bartholomew. London, 1923 (Shrewsbury Edition).
—— *Note-Books*, ed. Geoffrey Keynes and Brian Hill. London, 1951.
—— *Ernest Pontifex or The Way of All Flesh*, ed. Daniel F. Howard. New York, 1964.
Carpenter, Edward. *Civilization: Its Cause and Cure.* London, 1889.

—— *Intermediate Types Among Primitive Folk: A Study in Social Evolution*. London, 1914.

—— *Love's Coming of Age*. London, 1923.

—— *My Days and Dreams*. London, 1916.

—— *Towards Democracy*. London, 1923.

Caudwell, Christopher [Christopher St. John Sprigg]. *Studies in a Dying Culture*. London, 1938.

Clodd, Edward. *Thomas Henry Huxley*. Edinburgh and London, 1905.

Cohn, Saul. *Naturalisme et Mysticisme chez D. H. Lawrence*. Paris, 1932.

Corke, Helen. *D. H. Lawrence: The Croydon Years*. Austin, Tex., 1965.

Crews, Frederick C. *E. M. Forster: The Perils of Humanism*. Princeton, N.J., 1962.

Cunard, Nancy. *Grand Man*. London, 1916.

Darwin, Charles. *The Voyage of the Beagle*. London, 1906 (Everyman).

Dewey, John. *Experience and Nature*. New York, 1925.

D'Exideuil, Pierre. *The Human Pair in the Work of Thomas Hardy*. London, 1930.

Doughty, Charles M. *Adam Cast Forth*. London, 1908.

—— *Dawn in Britain*. 6 vols. London, 1906.

—— *Travels in Arabia Deserta*. 2 vols. London, 1924.

Douglas, Norman. *Experiments*. New York, 1925.

—— *Fountains in the Sand*. London, 1912.

—— *London Street Games*. London, 1916.

—— *Looking Back*. New York, 1933.

—— *Old Calabria*. London, 1938.

—— *On the Darwinian Hypothesis of Sexual Selection*. London, 1895.

—— *Paneros*. Florence, 1930.

—— *South Wind*. New York, 1960.

Duffin, Henry C. *Thomas Hardy: A Study of the Wessex Novels*. Manchester, 1937.

Eliot, Thomas Stearns. *After Strange Gods*. London, 1934.

—— *The Complete Poems and Plays 1909–1950*. New York, 1962.

—— *Selected Essays*. New York, 1932.

—— "Ulysses, Order, and Myth," *The Dial* (Nov 1923) 480–3.

Ellis, Havelock. "Concerning *Jude the Obscure*," *Ulysses Bookshop*. London, 1931.

—— *My Life*. Boston, 1939.

—— *The New Spirit*. London, 1890.

—— "Thomas Hardy's Novels," *Westminster Review*, CXIX (1 June 1883) 336–58.

Fahey, William A. *The Travel Books of D. H. Lawrence: Records of a Spiritual Journey*. Doctoral dissertation, English Department, New York University, 1964.

Fairchild, Hoxie Neale. "Rima's Mother," *PMLA*, LXVIII (1953) 357–70.

Fay, Eliot. *Lorenzo in Search of the Sun*. New York, 1953.

Fergusson, Francis. "D. H. Lawrence's Sensibility," *Critiques and Essays on Modern Fiction 1920–1951*, ed. John W. Aldredge. New York, 1952.

Firor, Ruth. *Folkways in Thomas Hardy*. Philadelphia, 1931.

Fletcher, J. V. "The Creator of Rima," *Sewanee Review*, XLI (1953) 24–40.

Ford, Ford Madox [Hueffer]. *The Good Soldier.* New York, 1951.
Forster, E. M. *Aspects of the Novel.* London, 1928.
—— *Howards End.* New York, 1944.
—— *The Longest Journey.* New York, 1922.
—— *A Passage to India.* New York, 1924.
—— *A Room with a View.* New York, 1961.
—— *Two Cheers for Democracy.* New York, 1951.
—— *Where Angels Fear to Tread.* New York, 1920.
Franc, Miriam A. *Ibsen in England.* New York, 1919.
Frazer, Sir James. *The Golden Bough.* 12 vols. London, 1890–1915.
Freud, Sigmund. *A General Introduction to Psycho-Analysis,* trans. J. Rivière. New York, 1953.
—— *Civilization and Its Discontents,* trans. James Strachey. New York, 1961.
—— *Collected Papers,* ed. J. Rivière and J. Strachey. 5 vols. New York and London, 1924–50.
Frierson, W. C. *The English Novel in Transition.* New York, 1942.
Furbank, P. N. *Samuel Butler.* Cambridge, 1948.
Galsworthy, John. *The Man of Property.* New York, 1922.
Gide, André. *Fruits of the Earth.* New York, 1949.
—— *If It Die,* trans. Dorothy Bussy. New York, 1935.
—— *Lafcadio's Adventures.* New York, 1928.
Graham, Robert Bontine Cunninghame. *Brought Forward.* London, 1917.
—— *Thirty Tales and Sketches by R. B. Cunninghame Graham,* ed. Edward Garnett. New York, 1929.
Granville-Barker, Harley. *The Eighteen Eighties.* Cambridge, 1930.
Gregory, Horace. *Pilgrim of the Apocalypse: A Critical Study of D. H. Lawrence.* New York, 1933.
Grimsditch, Herbert B. *Character and Environment in the Novels of Thomas Hardy.* London, 1925.
Grosskurth, Phyllis. *John Addington Symonds.* New York, 1964.
Guerard, Albert J. *André Gide.* New York, 1963.
—— *Joseph Conrad.* New York, 1947.
—— *Thomas Hardy: The Novels and Stories.* Cambridge, Mass., 1949.
Hamilton, Robert. *W. H. Hudson: The Vision of Earth.* London, 1946.
Hardy, Evelyn. *Thomas Hardy: A Critical Biography.* London, 1954.
—— *Thomas Hardy's Notebooks.* London, 1955.
Hardy, Florence Emily. *The Life of Thomas Hardy 1840–1928.* New York, 1962.
Hardy: A Collection of Critical Essays, ed. Albert J. Guerard. Englewood Cliffs, N.J., 1963 (Twentieth Century Views).
Hardy, Thomas. *Collected Poems of Thomas Hardy.* New York, 1961.
—— *"Dearest Emmie": Letters to His First Wife,* ed. Carl J. Weber. New York, 1963.
—— *The Dynasts.* London, 1923 (*The Poetical Works of Thomas Hardy,* vol. 2).
—— *Far From the Madding Crowd.* London, 1910.
—— *Jude the Obscure.* London, 1910.
—— *A Laodicean: A Story of Today.* London, 1910.
—— *Life and Art.* New York, 1925.
—— *The Mayor of Casterbridge: A Story of a Man of Character.* London, 1910.
—— *The Return of the Native.* London, 1910.

—— *Tess of the d'Urbervilles.* London, 1910.
—— *The Woodlanders.* London, 1910.
Harkness, Stanley B. *The Career of Samuel Butler: A Bibliography.* London, 1955.
Haymaker, Richard E. *From Pampas to Hedgerows and Downs: A Study of W. H. Hudson.* New York, 1954.
Henderson, Philip. *Samuel Butler: The Incarnate Bachelor.* London, 1953.
Henkin, Leo J. *Darwinism in the English Novel 1860–1910.* New York, 1940.
Henry James and H. G. Wells, ed. Leon Edel and Gordon Ray. Urbana, 1958.
Hoare, Dorothy M. "The Tragic in Hardy and Conrad," *Some Studies in the Modern Novel.* London, 1938.
Hoffman, Frederick J. *Freudianism and the Literary Mind.* Baton Rouge, 1945.
Holland, Norman Jr. "*Jude the Obscure*: Hardy's Symbolic Indictment of Christianity," *Nineteenth Century Fiction,* IX (June 1954) 50–60.
Holloway, John. *Jane Austen to Joseph Conrad.* Minneapolis, 1959.
Holt, Lee Albert. "E. M. Forster and Samuel Butler," *PMLA,* LXI (Sep. 1946) 804–19.
Hough, Graham. *The Dark Sun: A Study of D. H. Lawrence.* London, 1956.
Hudson, W. H. *Birds and Man.* New York, 1923.
—— *Birds of La Plata.* New York, 1923.
—— *Far Away and Long Ago: A History of My Early Life.* New York, 1923.
—— *Green Mansions.* New York, 1963.
—— *Idle Days in Patagonia.* New York, 1923.
—— *Letters to R. B. Cunninghame Graham,* ed. Richard Curle, London, 1941.
—— *A Little Boy Lost, Together with the Poems of W. H. Hudson.* New York, 1923 (Collected Works).
—— *The Naturalist in La Plata.* New York, 1923.
—— *153 Letters from W. H. Hudson 1901–1922,* ed. Edward Garnett. New York, 1923.
—— *The Purple Land.* New York, 1923.
—— *The Shepherd's Life.* New York, 1923.
Hughes, Glenn. *Imagism and the Imagists: A Study in Modern Poetry.* London, 1931.
Hulme, T. E. *Speculations.* London, 1924.
Huxley, Aldous. *The Doors of Perception.* New York, 1956.
—— *Point Counterpoint.* New York, 1928.
James, William. *Varieties of Religious Experience: A Study in Human Nature.* New York, 1902.
Johnson, S. F. "Hardy's and Burke's Sublime," *English Institute Essays 1958.* New York, 1959.
Jones, Ernest. *The Life and Work of Sigmund Freud.* 3 vols. New York, 1953–5.
Jones, Henry Festing. *Samuel Butler, Author of Erewhon: A Memoir.* London, 1919.
Joyce, James. *A Portrait of the Artist as a Young Man.* New York, 1963.
—— *Ulysses.* New York, 1922.
Kipling, Rudyard. *Kim.* New York, 1963.
—— *The Jungle Books.* New York, 1961.
—— *Plain Tales from the Hills.* New York, 1923.

—— *Something About Myself.* New York, 1937.
Kris, Ernst. *Psychoanalytic Explorations in Art.* New York, 1952.
Lawrence, David Herbert. *Aaron's Rod.* London, 1957 (Phoenix ed., vol. 3).
—— *The Complete Poems of D. H. Lawrence,* ed. Vivian de Sola Pinto and Warren Roberts. 2 vols. New York, 1964.
—— *The Complete Short Stories.* 3 vols. London, 1957 (Phoenix ed., vols. 11–13).
—— *Collected Letters,* ed. Harry T. Moore. New York, 1962.
—— *The Kangaroo.* London, 1957 (Phoenix ed., vol. 6).
—— *Lady Chatterley's Lover.* London, 1957 (Phoenix ed., vol. 10).
—— *The Letters of D. H. Lawrence,* ed. Aldous Huxley. London, 1932.
—— *The Lost Girl.* London, 1957 (Phoenix ed., vol. 8).
—— *Mornings in Mexico and Etruscan Places.* London, 1957 (Phoenix ed., vol. 18).
—— *Phoenix: The Posthumous Papers of D. H. Lawrence,* ed. Edward D. McDonald. New York, 1936.
—— *The Plumed Serpent.* London, 1957 (Phoenix ed., vol. 4).
—— *Pornography and Obscenity.* London, 1926.
—— *Psychoanalysis and the Unconscious and Fantasia of the Unconscious.* New York, 1960.
—— *The Rainbow.* London, 1957 (Phoenix ed., vol. 2).
—— *Reflections on the Death of a Porcupine.* Philadelphia, 1925.
—— *Sea and Sardinia.* London, 1957 (Phoenix ed., vol. 17).
—— *Sex, Literature, and Censorship,* ed. Harry T. Moore. New York, 1959.
—— *The Short Novels.* 2 vols. London, 1957 (Phoenix ed., vols. 14–15).
—— *Sons and Lovers.* London, 1957 (Phoenix ed., vol. 9).
—— *The Spirit of Place,* ed. Richard Aldington. London, 1935.
—— *The Trespasser.* London, 1957 (Phoenix ed., vol. 7).
—— *Twilight in Italy.* London, 1957 (Phoenix ed., vol. 16).
—— *The White Peacock.* London, 1957 (Phoenix ed., vol. 5).
—— *Women in Love.* London, 1957 (Phoenix ed., vol. 1).
—— *D. H. Lawrence's Letters to Bertrand Russell,* ed. Harry T. Moore, New York, 1948.
Lawrence, Frieda. *Not I But the Wind.* New York, 1934.
—— *The Memoirs and Correspondence,* ed. E. W. Tedlock. London, 1961.
Lawrence, T. E. *The Seven Pillars of Wisdom.* London, 1922.
Leavis, F. R. *D. H. Lawrence: Novelist.* New York, 1956.
—— *The Great Tradition.* New York, 1948.
Lewis, C. S. "Edmund Spenser: Introduction," *Modern British Writers,* ed. G. B. Harrison. New York, 1959, ɪ, 91–103.
Lillard, R. G. "Irony in Hardy and Conrad," *PMLA,* ʟ (Mar 1935) 316–22.
Lovejoy, A. O. "On the Discrimination of Romanticisms," *PMLA,* xxxɪx (1924) 229–53.
—— *Primitivism and Related Ideas in Antiquity.* Baltimore, 1935.
Luhan, Mabel Dodge. *Lorenzo in Taos.* London, 1933.
Mann, Thomas. "Freud and the Future," *Freud, Goethe, Wagner,* trans. H. T. Lowe-Porter. New York, 1937, pp. 3–45.
Marshall, William H. "*The Way of All Flesh*: The Dual Function of Edward Overton," *Texas Studies in Literature and Language,* ɪv (winter 1963) 583–90.

134   *Bibliography*

Maxwell, Donald. *The Landscape of Thomas Hardy.* London, 1934.
Miller, Joseph Hillis. *Thomas Hardy: Distance and Desire.* Cambridge, Mass., 1970.
Montaigne, Michel Eyquem de. *Essais,* ed. Raphael Pangaud. 2 vols. Paris, 1934.
Moore, George. *Esther Waters,* ed. Lionel Stevenson. Boston, 1963.
Moore, Harry T. *Poste Restante: A Lawrence Travel Calendar.* Berkeley, 1956.
—— *The Intelligent Heart.* New York, 1954.
More, Thomas. *Utopia,* ed. H. V. S. Ogden. New York, 1959.
Murry, John Middleton. *Son of Woman: The Story of D. H. Lawrence.* New York, 1931.
Nehls, Edward. *D. H. Lawrence: A Composite Biography.* 3 vols. Madison, 1957–9.
Nieman, Gilbert. "Thomas Hardy, Existentialist," *Twentieth Century Literature,* I (Jan 1956) 207–14.
Nietzsche, Friedrich. *The Birth of Tragedy and The Geneology of Morals,* trans. Francis Golffing. New York, 1956.
Orioli, G. *Adventures of a Bookseller.* Florence, 1937.
Pascal, Blaise. *Pensées.* London, 1943.
Pinto, Vivian de Sola. *D. H. Lawrence: Prophet of the Midlands.* Nottingham, 1951.
Pound, Ezra. "A Few Dont's by an Imagiste," *Poetry,* I (1913) 198–206.
Purdy, Richard L. *Thomas Hardy: A Bibliographical Study.* New York, 1954.
Rabelais, François. *Oeuvres.* 6 vols. Paris, 1913.
Ray, Gordon N. "The Early Novels of H. G. Wells," *The History of Mr. Polly.* New York, 1960.
Reinehr, Sister Mary Joan. *The Writings of Wilfrid Scawen Blunt: An Introduction and Study.* Milwaukee, 1940.
Richards, M. C. "Thomas Hardy's Ironic Vision," *Nineteenth Century Fiction,* III (Mar 1949) 265–79; IV (June 1949) 21–35.
Robbe-Grillet, Alain. "Old 'Values' and the New Novel," *Evergreen Review,* III, no. 9 (1959) 100–18.
Roberts, Morley. *Men, Books, and Birds.* London, 1925.
—— *W. H. Hudson: A Portrait.* London, 1924.
Rosenbaum, Sidonia C. "Bibliografia," *Guillermo Enrique Hudson.* New York, 1946 (Hispanic Institute Publication).
Rutland, William R. *Thomas Hardy: A Study of His Writings and Their Background.* New York, 1962.
Shaw, George Bernard. *The Quintessence of Ibsenism.* London, 1891.
—— *Selected Non-Dramatic Writings of Bernard Shaw,* ed. Dan H. Laurence. Boston, 1965.
—— Introduction, *The Way of All Flesh.* London, 1936 (World Classics).
Spender, Stephen. *The Destructive Element: A Study of Modern Writers and Beliefs.* Boston, 1935.
Spilka, Mark. *The Love Ethic of D. H. Lawrence.* Bloomington, Ind., 1955.
Stanford, Raney. "Thomas Hardy and Lawrence's *The White Peacock,*" *MFS,* V (spring 1959) 19–28.
Stewart, J. I. M. *Eight Modern Writers.* Oxford, 1963 (Oxford History of English Literature).

Surtz, Rev. Edward L. *The Praise of Pleasure: Philosophy, Education, and Communism in More's Utopia*. New York, 1957.

Swift, Jonathan. *Gulliver's Travels*. New York, 1933.

Swinnerton, Frank. *The Georgian Literary Scene 1910–1935*. New York, 1937.

Synge, John M. *The Aran Islands*. London and Dublin, 1907.

Thomalin, Ruth. *W. H. Hudson*. New York, 1954.

Tillyard, E. M. W. *Myth and the English Mind from Piers Plowman to Edward Gibbon*. New York, 1961.

Tiverton, Father William Martin Jarrett-Kerr. *D. H. Lawrence and Human Existence*. London, 1951.

Tomkins, J. M. *The Art of Rudyard Kipling*. London, 1959.

Tomlinson, Henry Major. *Norman Douglas*. London, 1952 (rev. ed.).

—— *The Sea and the Jungle*. New York, 1961.

Trilling, Diana. Introduction, *The Portable D. H. Lawrence*. New York, 1947.

Trilling, Lionel. *E. M. Forster*. Norfolk, 1943.

—— *Freud and the Crisis of Our Culture*. Boston, 1955.

Valentin, Antonina. *H. G. Wells: Prophet of Our Day*. New York, 1950.

Van Ghent, Dorothy. *The English Novel: Form and Function*. New York, 1953.

Vivas, Eliseo. *D. H. Lawrence: The Failure and the Triumph of Art*. Evanston, 1960.

Waugh, Evelyn. *A Handful of Dust*. New York, 1961.

Webster, Harvey Curtis. *On a Darkling Plain*. Chicago, 1947.

Wells, H. G. *Experiment in Autobiography*. London, 1934.

—— *The History of Mr. Polly*, ed. Gordon N. Ray. Boston, 1960.

—— *Tono-Bungay*. New York, 1960.

White, William. *D. H. Lawrence: A Checklist*. Detroit, 1950.

Whitehead, Alfred North. *Science and the Modern World*. New York, 1925.

Wilde, Alan. *Art and Order: A Study of E. M. Forster*. New York, 1964.

Williams, William Carlos. *The Complete Collected Poems of William Carlos Williams 1906–1937*. Norfolk, 1938.

Wilson, G. F. *A Bibliography of the Writings of W. H. Hudson*. London, 1922.

Woolf, Cecil. *A Bibliography of Norman Douglas*. London, 1954.

Wright, Raymond. "Lawrence's Non-Human Analogues," *MLN*, LXXVI (May 1955) 426–32.

Yeats, William Butler. *Selected Poems and Two Plays of William Butler Yeats*, ed. M. L. Rosenthal. New York, 1962.

—— *Letters of W. B. Yeats*, ed. Allan Wade. New York, 1955.

Youman, Ida K. *D. H. Lawrence: His Criticism of the "Study of Thomas Hardy."* Master's thesis, (English Department), New York University, 1955.

Zabel, Morton Dauwen. *Craft and Character in Modern Fiction*. New York, 1940.

Index